Contents

Introduction

snowflakes
slip from the sky
like soft white butterflies

"I love reading poetry with my students, but I just don't know how to teach them to read a poem and respond to it." Are you one of countless teachers who share this sentiment? If so, the simple, structured lessons of *Read and Understand Poetry* are just what you need!

- Easy-to-follow lessons guide you in introducing and reading poems chosen especially for students at your grade level.

- Quick and easy minilessons help you work with your students on the language arts skills that are unique to poetry.

- Individual follow-up activity pages help students consolidate what they have learned and extend their critical thinking and creativity.

What's on the Teacher Page?

The **teacher page** provides a simple, easy-to-follow lesson plan that includes these features:

The **Before You Read** section provides important background information for you to share with students prior to reading the poem. Guidelines for developing key concepts and suggestions for preteaching vocabulary are found here.

The **While You Read** section helps you choose the best way for students to experience each poem for the first time (such as listening to you read it aloud, reading it aloud chorally or individually, reading it silently, etc.).

The **After You Read** section guides you in presenting minilessons that focus on different types of poetry and on important elements of the language arts curriculum for poetry.

What's on the Poem Page?

Each **poem page** presents:

- the text of the poetry featured in the lesson

- a simple illustration to enhance comprehension

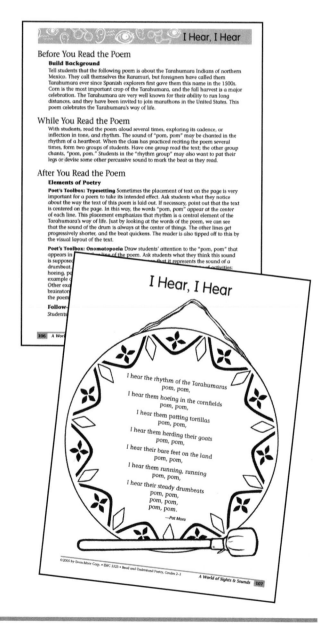

snowflakes
slip from the sky
like soft white butterflies

What's on the Follow-up Activity Pages?

As you guide students through the lessons outlined on the teacher page, they will have multiple opportunities to work as part of a group on developing an understanding of the form and content of each poem. The Follow-up Activities give students the opportunity to synthesize new information and practice language arts skills introduced during teacher-directed minilessons.

The first page of **Follow-up Activities** is designed to help students consolidate their comprehension of the poem by having them select the only correct response out of four possible choices for each of these multiple-choice items. Item content covers:

- literal comprehension

- sequence

- word meanings

- context clues and inferences

- main idea and details

In addition, the item format on this first activity page emulates the format students are likely to encounter on standardized language arts tests. After completing the activity pages in *Read and Understand Poetry*, students will be undaunted when a poem is presented as a reading passage on their next standardized test.

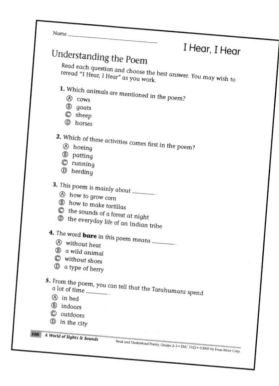

The second page of **Follow-up Activities** may focus on any aspect of the language arts curriculum touched upon in the poem. Students may be invited to share their opinions as they respond to open-ended questions, to try their hand at using poetic techniques such as onomatopoeia or alliteration, or to write a poem of their own. Critical thinking and creativity are encouraged on this type of activity page.

Snowflakes
slip from the sky
like soft white butterflies

What Are the Additional Student Resources?

A seven-page **Glossary of Poetry Terms** features kid-friendly definitions and pronunciation guidelines for terms ranging from *alliteration* to *simile*. Each glossary entry includes an example drawn from this anthology, further strengthening students' connection to poetry terminology.

An **About the Poets** feature presents brief, high-interest information on each of the poets included in this anthology. This helps build the additional context that allows students to deepen their understanding of the work of specific poets.

Designed for classroom display, the **Poetry Posters** present key elements and forms of poetry in a clear graphic format.

How to Use These Materials

To create a unique poetry anthology for your students, reproduce for each student:

- the cover page for the student *Read & Understand Poetry Anthology*

- the table of contents for each unit

- the poem and follow-up activity pages for each poem

- the Glossary of Poetry Terms and About the Poets pages

Place these pages together in a folder or three-ring binder to create individual poetry anthologies.

As students encounter new poems in their ongoing reading, they can use this resource to help them enjoy and deepen their knowledge of this timeless art form.

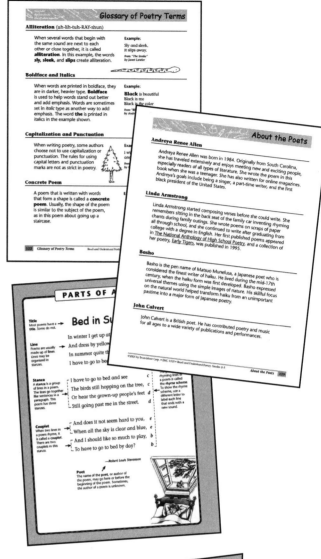

Beasts, Birds, & Bugs

Contents

Before You Read the Poem

Build Background

Invite students to share what they know about ladybugs, including information such as how they look, where they live, how they move, and what they eat. You may wish to point out that ladybugs are beneficial insects that eat other tiny insect pests that harm plants. For this reason, gardeners are usually happy to see ladybugs in their gardens.

Tell students that they will read a poem that is similar to an old-fashioned nursery rhyme about a ladybug. Invite volunteers to recite the verse if it is familiar, or share the following version with students: *Ladybug, ladybug/Fly away home./Your house is on fire/And your children all gone./All except one,/And that's little Ann./She has crept under the warming pan.*

Compare Real and Imaginary Ladybugs

Review the traditional rhyme with children and use prompts to help elicit information about elements of the poem that could really happen and those that are imaginary: *Could a ladybug really fly home? Do ladybugs really live in houses?*, etc.

While You Read the Poem

Encourage students to listen closely for the poet's message to the ladybug in this modern version of the poem. Then invite students to follow along as you read the poem aloud.

After You Read the Poem

Elements of Poetry

Poet's Toolbox: Innovation Explain to students that sometimes authors create new works that are based upon existing ones. In this case, John Himmelman uses a traditional rhyme for a springboard to a new, fun poem about ladybugs. A new poem made this way is called an *innovation*.

Poet's Toolbox: Personification Ask children to consider whether the actions described could actually be carried out by ladybugs. Elicit from students the idea that the author is attributing human characteristics to the ladybugs in the poem. This is called *personification*. You may wish to brainstorm other examples of familiar stories where animals or other nonhuman characters have human characteristics and behaviors, such as *Goldilocks and the Three Bears, The Little Engine That Could,* and others.

Follow-up Activities

Students may work independently to complete the activities on pages 8 and 9.

Ladybug, Ladybug

Ladybug, Ladybug
Stay right here.
Don't fly home,
You have nothing to fear.

Your children are sleeping.
Your husband is shopping.
Your father is sweeping.
Your mother is mopping.

Your grandma is strumming.
Your grandpa is clapping.
Your auntie is humming.
Your uncle is napping.

Your brother is riding.
Your sister is cooking.
Your niece is hiding.
Your nephew is looking.

Ladybug, Ladybug
Stay right here.
Don't fly home,
You have nothing to fear.

—*John Himmelman*

Ladybug, Ladybug

Understanding the Poem

Read each question and choose the best answer. You may wish to reread "Ladybug, Ladybug" as you work.

1. In the poem, what is the father ladybug doing?
- Ⓐ cooking
- Ⓑ clapping
- Ⓒ jumping
- Ⓓ sweeping

2. Which family member is mentioned last in the poem?
- Ⓐ sister
- Ⓑ uncle
- Ⓒ nephew
- Ⓓ mother

3. Which word in the poem describes the action used in playing a guitar?
- Ⓐ strumming
- Ⓑ mopping
- Ⓒ napping
- Ⓓ sleeping

4. What does the speaker want the ladybug to do?
- Ⓐ fly away
- Ⓑ sing a song
- Ⓒ crawl around
- Ⓓ stay where she is

5. How does the speaker want the ladybug to feel?
- Ⓐ angry
- Ⓑ calm
- Ⓒ afraid
- Ⓓ excited

Understanding the Poem

1. List 3 pairs of rhyming words from the poem.

_____   _____   _____

_____   _____   _____

Write one more word that rhymes with each pair.

_____   _____   _____

2. Find the words in the poem that name family members.
Write them here.

_____   _____   _____

_____   _____   _____

_____   _____   _____

_____   _____   _____

3. Use **-ing** words to make a list of things that you might see
a ladybug doing.

_____   _____   _____

_____   _____   _____

4. Draw a picture of a ladybug doing something from your list.

Before You Read the Poem

Build Background

Tell students that poets often use the sounds of words to help bring the subject of a poem to life. Explain that they will be hearing a poem called "The Snake." Invite students to speculate about the sounds a poet might use to help make the snake in the poem come alive.

Introduce Sound Words

Have students repeat these words after you: *slick and silent, slow and sliding, sly and sleek, slithers and slips.* Guide students in noting how the pairs of words begin with the same sound *(sl)* and how this sound is similar to a snake's hissing. Ask students to listen to the way these words are used in the poem.

While You Read the Poem

Invite students to listen as you read the poem aloud. Then ask them to follow along as you read the poem again, underlining words that begin with the initial *s* sound. Have some volunteers share the words they underlined; others may read the poem aloud. You or a student might list the words on the board; point out how the shape of the *s* even looks like a snake.

After You Read the Poem

Elements of Poetry

Poet's Toolbox: Rhyme Ask students to circle words in the poem that rhyme *(toe/go; glide/hide; know/so; away/today)*. Tell students that poets often use rhyme to lighten the mood of what might otherwise be a serious poem. In "The Snake," for example, readers are never frightened that the speaker will be bitten because the irregular rhyme scheme contributes to an almost singsong recitation.

Poet's Toolbox: Alliteration Remind students that poets use sound in many special ways to help make their poems come alive. When a poet puts several words that begin with the same consonant sound close to each other in a poem, it is called *alliteration*. Point out *slick* and *silent* in the first line, then encourage students to find other instances of alliteration in the poem.

Explain how the repetition of the initial *s* sound paints a sound picture of the snake as it moves through the grass, close to the speaker's foot. Note that the words *slow, sliding,* and *slithers* evoke suspense as readers wait to see what the snake will do. In the second half of the poem, the number of *s* sounds increases, reflecting the movement of the snake as it slips swiftly away.

Follow-up Activities

Students may work independently to complete the activities on pages 12 and 13.

The Snake

Slick and silent,
near my toe,
through the leaves,
I see it go.
Over sticks
I watch it glide,
looking for a place to hide.
Slow and sliding,
does it know,
I'm scared of how it
slithers so?
Sly and sleek,
it slips away.
I'm glad it passed me by
today!

—Janet Lawler

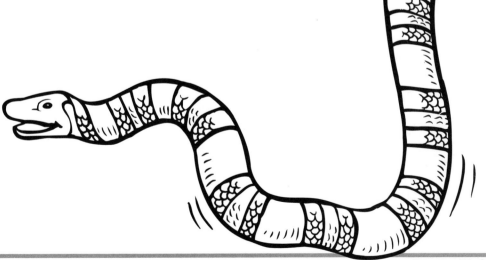

Understanding the Poem

Read each question and choose the best answer. You may wish to reread "The Snake" as you work.

1. What **slithers** in this poem?

Ⓐ leaves

Ⓑ a snake

Ⓒ a worm

Ⓓ the speaker

2. What is the snake trying to do?

Ⓐ dig a hole

Ⓑ climb a tree

Ⓒ find a place to hide

Ⓓ make its way home

3. How do you think the speaker feels about snakes?

Ⓐ tired

Ⓑ upset

Ⓒ happy

Ⓓ afraid

4. Which of the following does <u>not</u> mean the same as **sleek**?

Ⓐ rough

Ⓑ shiny

Ⓒ silky

Ⓓ smooth

5. How does the speaker feel when the snake is gone?

Ⓐ sad

Ⓑ angry

Ⓒ happy

Ⓓ disappointed

Name _____

Understanding the Poem

1. "The Snake" has many words that begin with the sound of the letter **s**. Read each word. Circle the words that begin with the **s** sound. Be careful! Some words that begin with the **s** sound may be spelled with a different letter!

snake	cycle	sack	cob
city	cry	count	center
slither	circle	sly	safe

2. Some of the words in "The Snake" rhyme. Find words in the poem that rhyme with each of these words, or add rhyming words of your own.

toe	glide	away
_____	_____	_____
_____	_____	_____

3. When a poet puts words that begin with the same consonant sound near each other in a poem, we call it **alliteration**. Find four lines in "The Snake" that include alliteration. Write the two words from each line below.

_____, _____

_____, _____

_____, _____

_____, _____

4. Snakes are just one type of creature you might see outside. Write a complete sentence about other animals, birds, or insects you might see outside.

_____

_____

_____

Before You Read the Poem

Build Background

Explain to students that a swallow is a small bird that is often associated with the coming of spring. You might show them the picture of the swallow on page 15.

Talk with students about the seasonal migration of many birds, including swallows. Typically, birds fly to warmer areas at the approach of winter and return with springtime. Depending on where you live, you may be able to help students identify some birds that commonly migrate in or out of your area.

About the Poet

Christina Rossetti was born in England in 1830. She was a shy young woman who was raised in a very literate and artistic family. She lived a quiet and religious life; she never married. She wrote many poems throughout her life.

While You Read the Poem

Read the poem aloud, expressively. Guide students in a discussion of the feeling expressed by the poem. Students should understand that the writer is sad to see the departure of the swallow at the end of summer, and longingly looks forward to the swallow's return.

After You Read the Poem

Elements of Poetry

Form: Lyric Poetry Lyric poetry focuses on emotional expression. Lyric poems may be long and elaborate or short and simple, as this one is. The emotion expressed in a lyric poem often prompts the reader to reflect on a similar feeling or experience.

Poet's Toolbox: Alliteration Remind students that alliteration is the repetition of initial consonant sounds in words that are in close proximity. An example is "sun-loving swallow," which appears in the second line of the poem. Also point out occurrences of words starting with the same letter that don't appear side by side, such as "Come again, come again, come back to me."

Ask students to find examples of alliteration in each line.

Follow-up Activities

Students may work independently to complete the activities on pages 16 and 17.

Fly Away, Fly Away

Fly away, fly away over the sea,
Sun-loving swallow, for summer is done;
Come again, come again, come back to me,
Bringing the summer, and bringing the sun.

—*Christina Rossetti*

Beasts, Birds, & Bugs **15**

Understanding the Poem

Read each question and choose the best answer. You may wish to reread "Fly Away, Fly Away" as you work.

1. Which season of the year is mentioned in the poem?

Ⓐ winter

Ⓑ spring

Ⓒ summer

Ⓓ fall

2. The swallow is described as _____ .

Ⓐ happy

Ⓑ kind

Ⓒ beautiful

Ⓓ sun-loving

3. Why does the swallow fly away?

Ⓐ because summer is over

Ⓑ because it is hungry

Ⓒ because it is lonely

Ⓓ because it is sad

4. The word **sea** means _____ .

Ⓐ mountain

Ⓑ ocean

Ⓒ look

Ⓓ rain

5. You can tell from this poem that the poet _____ .

Ⓐ wants the swallow to come back

Ⓑ wants to go with the swallow

Ⓒ does not like the swallow

Ⓓ likes cold weather

Understanding the Poem

1. How do you think the poet feels about summer?

_____

_____

2. In this poem, the poet thinks about the swallow and the summertime as two things that appear together. List some of the things that might appear together during each season.

summer _____

fall _____

spring _____

winter _____

3. What is your favorite season of the year? _____
Draw a picture to illustrate what you like about this season.

Before You Read the Poem

Build Background

This poem brings to mind the ponies of Chincoteague and Assateague Islands off Virginia. Children may be familiar with them through *Misty of Chincoteague*, Marguerite Henry's classic children's book that helped to popularize these delightful ponies. If not, tell children that people believe that these horses were brought to the area on Spanish ships over 400 years ago. When storms wrecked the ships, the horses escaped from the cargo holds and swam to shore. Over the years, the ponies adapted to the coastal environment, becoming a small, sturdy breed. Learn more about the Chincoteague ponies at the following Web site: http://www.imh.org/imh/bw/chinco.html.

While You Read the Poem

Have students read the poem silently to themselves. Next, model a partner reading of the poem by asking a student to read the initial line of each of the first three stanzas ("I would love to be a horse") while you respond with the next two lines. Read the fourth stanza together. Finally, pair students to practice this partner reading. Encourage volunteers to share their reading with the group.

After You Read the Poem

Elements of Poetry

Form: Free Verse Tell students that in some poems, there are no pairs of rhyming words and no pattern of meter, or rhythm. This type of poem is called *free verse*. Poets who write in free verse have other ways to make their words "sound" like poetry. In this poem, repeating patterns are used to help set it apart from prose. Have students find the repeating patterns in the poem (the initial lines in stanzas 1 through 3 and the descriptions of actions in the remainder of each of those stanzas).

Poet's Toolbox: Imagery The poet uses powerful visual and sensory images in this poem. The reader can almost feel the cool ocean breeze and the texture of firm, wet sand; you can almost hear the sound of galloping hoofbeats and pounding waves. Invite students to try to make a picture of the scene in their mind as they listen to or read the poem again.

Follow-up Activities

Students may work independently to complete the activities on pages 20 and 21.

I Would Love to Be a Horse

I would love to be a horse;
to race along the shore,
the wind in my mane.

I would love to be a horse;
to skim the sand
with beating hooves.

I would love to be a horse;
to rear up and challenge
the thundering surf.

Galloping below wild cliffs,
all my muscles would sing,
"I am alive."

—Linda Armstrong

Name _____

Understanding the Poem

Read each question and choose the best answer. You may wish to reread "I Would Love to Be a Horse" as you work.

1. The poet would like to be _____ .

- (A) a cat
- (B) a cow
- (C) a horse
- (D) a donkey

2. In this poem, the word **surf** means _____ .

- (A) ocean waves
- (B) riding waves
- (C) small pebbles
- (D) collecting shells

3. This poem is mostly about horses _____ .

- (A) standing in the sun
- (B) sleeping in the barn
- (C) eating in the pasture
- (D) running on the beach

4. The word **hooves** refers to the horse's _____ .

- (A) ears
- (B) feet
- (C) eyes
- (D) mane

5. Galloping is another word for _____ .

- (A) resting
- (B) trotting
- (C) running
- (D) walking

Read and Understand Poetry • EMC 3323 • ©2005 by Evan-Moor Corp.

Name _____

Understanding the Poem

1. **Verbs** are words that tell about actions. These are some of the verbs in the poem that tell about some of the horse's actions: **race**, **rear**, **gallop**. Write some other verbs to describe a horse's actions.

   _____

   _____

   _____

2. If you could be any animal, what animal would you like to be?

   _____

3. What are some verbs that describe the action of this animal?

   _____

   _____

4. Draw a picture of the animal you would like to be.

   Write a sentence explaining what the animal in the picture is doing.

   _____

   _____

Before You Read the Poem

Build Background and Vocabulary

Tell students the poem they will read next is called "The Spider and the Fly." Invite them to share what they know about why spiders spin webs. Be sure to mention that spiders spin very sticky webs in order to catch flies and other insects. Spiders eat these insects for nourishment. Tell students that many years ago, the room where people brought guests for talking and visiting was called a *parlour*. Point out that the word is spelled without the *u* in America *(parlor)* and with it in England.

Review Anthropomorphic Characters

Remind students that in many stories, animals, insects, or toys talk and think just the way people do. Invite students to share some examples, such as characters in *A Bug's Life, Toy Story, Charlotte's Web,* or *Pinocchio.* Point out that even though such creatures can't truly talk and think like people, poets and other writers often use these characters as a fun way to show how real people sometimes behave. Ask children to pay attention to the way the two characters in this poem act.

While You Read the Poem

Remind students that this poem involves a conversation between a spider and a fly. Assign volunteers to read the lines for the narrator, the spider, and the fly in the first four stanzas of the poem. Choose several others to read the narrator's lines in three of the last four stanzas of the poem.

After You Read the Poem

Elements of Poetry

Poet's Toolbox: Dialog Tell students that a dialog is a conversation between two or more people. When authors write dialog, they usually use quotation marks to show the words that are spoken by each character. Invite students to find the quotation marks in this poem.

Follow-up Activities

Students may work independently to complete the activities on pages 25 and 26.

You may wish to have students explore the poem's central concept of flattery further. First, make sure students understand that *flattery* is excessive or false praise given as part of an effort to gain favor with the person being flattered. Then encourage interested learners to explore more about flattery. You might provide a version of Aesop's fable "The Fox and the Crow" so students may compare the flattery used in each tale. Encourage them to discuss why flattery works so well.

The Spider and the Fly

A New Version of an Old Story.

1 "Will you walk into my parlour?" said the Spider to the Fly,
"'Tis the prettiest little parlour that ever you did spy;
The way into my parlour is up a winding stair,
And I've many curious things to show when you are there."
"Oh no, no," said the little Fly, "to ask me is in vain,
For who goes up your winding stair can ne'er come down again."

2 "I'm sure you must be weary, dear, with soaring up so high;
Will you rest upon my little bed?" said the Spider to the Fly.
"There are pretty curtains drawn around; the sheets are fine and thin,
And if you like to rest awhile, I'll snugly tuck you in!"
"Oh no, no," said the little Fly, "for I've often heard it said,
They never, never wake again, who sleep upon your bed!"

3 Said the cunning Spider to the Fly, "Dear friend what can I do,
To prove the warm affection I've always felt for you?
I have within my pantry, good store of all that's nice;
I'm sure you're very welcome—will you please to take a slice?"
"Oh no, no," said the little Fly, "kind sir, that cannot be,
I've heard what's in your pantry, and I do not wish to see!"

4 "Sweet creature!" said the Spider, "you're witty and you're wise,
How handsome are your gauzy wings, how brilliant are your eyes!
I've a little looking-glass upon my parlour shelf,
If you'll step in one moment, dear, you shall behold yourself."
"I thank you, gentle sir," she said, "for what you're pleased to say,
And bidding you good morning now, I'll call another day."

5 The Spider turned him round about, and went into his den,
   For well he knew the silly Fly would soon come back again:
   So he wove a subtle web, in a little corner sly,
   And set his table ready, to dine upon the Fly.
   Then he came out to his door again, and merrily did sing,

6 "Come hither, hither, pretty Fly, with the pearl and silver wing;
   Your robes are green and purple—there's a crest upon your head;
   Your eyes are like the diamond bright, but mine are dull as lead!"

7 Alas, alas! How very soon this silly little Fly,
   Hearing his wily, flattering words, came slowly flitting by;
   With buzzing wings she hung aloft, then near and nearer drew,
   Thinking only of her brilliant eyes, and green and purple hue—
   Thinking only of her crested head—poor foolish thing! At last,
   Up jumped the cunning Spider, and fiercely held her fast.
   He dragged her up his winding stair, into his dismal den,
   Within his little parlour—but she ne'er came out again!

8 And now dear little children, who may this story read,
   To idle, silly flattering words, I pray you ne'er give heed:
   Unto an evil counselor, close heart and ear and eye,
   And take a lesson from this tale, of the Spider and the Fly.

—*Mary Howitt*

Understanding the Poem

Read each question and choose the best answer. You may wish to reread "The Spider and the Fly" as you work.

1. What does the poet think about the spider and the fly?
- Ⓐ Neither of them is very smart.
- Ⓑ The spider is smarter than the fly.
- Ⓒ The fly is smarter than the spider.
- Ⓓ The spider and the fly are both very smart.

2. At the end, why did the fly return to the spider's parlour?
- Ⓐ She was very brave.
- Ⓑ She thought she would be safe.
- Ⓒ She wanted to sit on the lovely furniture.
- Ⓓ She started to believe the spider's compliments.

3. What is the main idea of this poem?
- Ⓐ Flies are vain and foolish.
- Ⓑ Don't let a spider trick you.
- Ⓒ Don't be fooled by flattering remarks.
- Ⓓ You should be polite to those who flatter you.

4. In stanza 5, what does the spider do after the fly leaves?
- Ⓐ spins a new web
- Ⓑ sits and sulks in his den
- Ⓒ puts some flowers in a vase
- Ⓓ invites another fly to come in

5. What is another name for **looking-glass**?
- Ⓐ magnifying glass
- Ⓑ contact lens
- Ⓒ microscope
- Ⓓ mirror

The Spider and the Fly

Understanding the Poem

1. **Synonyms** are words that have the same meanings. Circle the synonym for the underlined word in each sentence.

   a. The cunning spider was very <u>tricky</u>.

         clever   deadly   speedy

   b. The fly's crest was very <u>handsome</u>.

         bright   lovely   expensive

   c. The spider's <u>flattery</u> tricked the fly.

         jokes   confusion   compliments

2. How else might the spider have tricked the fly into entering the parlour? Think of another good idea, then write it below. Use complete sentences to explain your idea.

   _____

   _____

   _____

3. Imagine that you are a smart fly. The spider cannot trick you with flattery. What will you say to the spider? What new tricks will he try to use on you? Write a short dialog to show the words you each would say.

Seasons & Celebrations

Contents

Before You Read the Poem

Build Background

Explain to students that many ancient cultures celebrated the New Year on the first of April, possibly because it closely followed the vernal equinox. In 1582, a new calendar was put into place, and New Year's Day moved to January 1. In France, many people refused to accept the new calendar, so they continued to celebrate the New Year on April 1. These people soon became known as "April Fools," and they often found themselves the victims of good-natured pranks. Playing small, harmless tricks on one another is a custom still practiced on what is now known as April Fools' Day.

Activate Prior Knowledge

Ask partners to recall harmless April Fools' Day tricks they have played on others, then share some recollections with the group. Make sure students understand that April Fools' Day tricks should be harmless jokes or tricks made in the spirit of fun. (If examples of inappropriate tricks are shared, be sure to guide students in identifying the reasons such pranks are inappropriate.)

While You Read the Poem

Direct students to read the poem silently, then to reread and circle the rhyming words. Invite volunteers to read the poem aloud and then share the words they circled. You or a volunteer may write each pair of rhyming words on the board.

After You Read the Poem

Elements of Poetry

Poet's Toolbox: Rhyme and Rhythm Ask students to brainstorm reasons why poets sometimes use rhyme. Guide them to an understanding that rhyme helps spoken words sound musical. Rhythm, the sound of accented and unaccented syllables, also contributes to a musical quality in verse. To demonstrate, ask a volunteer to read an example of how "April's Trick" might sound if rhyme and rhythm were not used: *There's a bug on your back,/It's green and yellow./You've got spots on your face./I'll bet you haven't seen them.*

Poet's Toolbox: Meter Tell students that a regular pattern of rhythm is known as *meter*. Poetic language that uses meter is called *verse*. Language that does not make use of meter is called *prose*. Give examples of prose that students have read with you in class to help clarify the distinction between poetry and prose. Highlight the regular meter of poetry as you contrast text types.

Follow-up Activities

Students may work independently to complete the activities on pages 30 and 31.

April's Trick

There's a bug on your back,
And it's yellow and green.
You've spots on your face
I'll bet you've not seen.
There's a rip in your coat,
And your hair's turning gray.
Don't get upset though,
It's April Fools' Day.

—*Martin Shaw*

Understanding the Poem

Read each question and choose the best answer. You may wish to reread "April's Trick" as you work.

1. According to the poem, what's wrong with the coat?
- Ⓐ It's inside out.
- Ⓑ It's too big.
- Ⓒ It's ripped.
- Ⓓ It's ugly.

2. According to the poem, what color is the bug?
- Ⓐ blue and gray
- Ⓑ red and orange
- Ⓒ brown and black
- Ⓓ yellow and green

3. When does the poem take place?
- Ⓐ April 1
- Ⓑ April 15
- Ⓒ January 1
- Ⓓ December 25

4. Why shouldn't the person in the poem get upset?
- Ⓐ because the spots will disappear
- Ⓑ because the coat can be mended
- Ⓒ because the bug is not dangerous
- Ⓓ because the bad things aren't true

5. What is this poem mainly about?
- Ⓐ a coat that got ripped
- Ⓑ an odd bug that appeared one day
- Ⓒ an April Fools' joke that someone played
- Ⓓ someone who got sick with an odd illness

Understanding the Poem

1. Some of the words in the poem "April's Trick" rhyme. Practice your rhyming skills by writing three words that rhyme with each word given.

green   **gray**

_____   _____

_____   _____

_____   _____

2. Complete the poem below by filling in the blanks. Then draw a picture to illustrate your poem.

If I had to choose

The best holiday,

I would pick _____

Any old day.

I get to _____

And to have lots of fun.

That is why _____

Is my favorite one.

I chose this day

Above all the rest

Because _____

_____

And because _____

_____

Before You Read the Poem

Build Background

Ask students to think about the difference between the time of nightfall in summer and in winter. Explain to students that this difference becomes greater the nearer one lives to the Earth's poles. For example, Sweden is sometimes called "The Land of the Midnight Sun" because in summer the sun barely sets at all. Ask students to describe what the light was like when they got up this morning and when they went to bed last night.

About the Poet

Tell students that Robert Louis Stevenson was born and raised in Scotland (you may wish to point out Scotland on a map or globe). Share this information on Stevenson's life: He was his parents' only child and was a sickly child, so he spent more time in bed than most children; he loved to write, and first published his writing as a teenager. Students may be familiar with Stevenson's famous novel *Treasure Island*. Let them know that he also wrote poetry for children, and the next poem they will read is from his collection *A Child's Garden of Verses*.

While You Read the Poem

Set the stage for the poem. Ask the children to imagine lying in bed while it is still light outside. Have them picture the bed by a window through which they can see trees and birds. The open window is on the second floor of a house, high above a city street. The sounds of people passing by can be heard from below. Allow children to stretch out on the floor if your classroom can accommodate this.

Tell the children that you are going to read them a poem that describes the thoughts that might float through a child's mind in such a situation.

After You Read the Poem

Elements of Poetry

Form: Couplets Guide students in locating the rhyming words at the end of each pair of lines in the poem. Explain to students that pairs of rhyming lines are called *couplets*. Write the word on the board and ask them to find within it a more familiar word that means "two." *(couple)*

Follow-up Activities

Students may work independently to complete the activities on pages 34 and 35.

Students may enjoy reading more poetry by Robert Louis Stevenson. Encourage them to enjoy other poems from his famous collection, *A Child's Garden of Verses*. There are many editions in print, or access this poetry online at sites including this one: http://www.poetryloverspage.com.

Bed in Summer

In winter I get up at night
And dress by yellow candle-light.
In summer quite the other way,
I have to go to bed by day.

I have to go to bed and see
The birds still hopping on the tree,
Or hear the grown-up people's feet
Still going past me in the street.

And does it not seem hard to you,
When all the sky is clear and blue,
And I should like so much to play,
To have to go to bed by day?

—Robert Louis Stevenson

Understanding the Poem

Read each question and choose the best answer. You may wish to reread "Bed in Summer" as you work.

1. What animals does the child in the poem see from the bedroom window?

   Ⓐ squirrels

   Ⓑ rabbits

   Ⓒ birds

   Ⓓ cows

2. This poem is mainly about _____.

   Ⓐ a child's feelings about bedtime

   Ⓑ animals that live in the city

   Ⓒ a winter day

   Ⓓ clouds

3. The child does <u>not</u> want to _____.

   Ⓐ eat dinner

   Ⓑ do homework

   Ⓒ play outside with friends

   Ⓓ go to bed while it's still light outside

4. The word **hopping** in the poem means _____.

   Ⓐ sliding

   Ⓑ sleeping

   Ⓒ jumping

   Ⓓ swimming

5. You can tell from the poem that the child can hear _____.

   Ⓐ a band playing

   Ⓑ people passing by

   Ⓒ a baby crying

   Ⓓ dogs barking

Understanding the Poem

1. Write three pairs of rhyming words from the poem.

_____ , _____

_____ , _____

_____ , _____

2. Finish this sentence:
If I looked out the window just before going to bed, I might see

_____

_____

_____

3. The child in the poem would like to stay up and play. Write a sentence that tells what you think the child would like to do.

_____

_____

4. Draw a picture to illustrate your sentence.

Before You Read the Poem

Build Background

Ask students to name an important holiday that takes place in the month of July (Independence Day, July 4th). Discuss some of the ways that we celebrate this holiday. If your students are unfamiliar with these traditions, the following resources can deepen their understanding:

- *Fourth of July Story* by Alice Dalgliesh
- *Hooray for the Fourth of July* by Wendy Watson
- http://www.twighlightbridge.com

Activate Prior Knowledge

Help students connect the theme of this poem to their personal experiences by inviting them to share about a favorite Fourth of July experience. You may need to start things out by sharing a story of your own. Then allow time for students to talk about how their families celebrate this holiday.

While You Read the Poem

Read the poem aloud, emphasizing the sound words. Pair students and ask partners to take turns reading the poem to each other. Allow volunteers to read the poem to the class, again emphasizing the sound words.

After You Read the Poem

Elements of Poetry

Poet's Toolbox: Internal Rhymes Point out to students that the first line of each stanza in this poem is made up of two rhyming words. Most rhyming poems feature rhyming words at the end of each line, but often there are rhymes within lines as well. These are called *internal rhymes*. Students may also notice that the last word on the second line also rhymes with these words. Do they notice any other rhyme patterns?

Poet's Toolbox: Onomatopoeia When we use words that imitate the sounds they describe, it is called *onomatopoeia*. Offer several examples (such as *hiss, pop, buzz*), then encourage students to find other examples in the poem (*crunch, sizzle, booming*). Brainstorm other examples of onomatopoeia, such as *bang, slurp, ding*, and more.

Follow-up Activities

Students may work independently to complete the activities on pages 38 and 39.

Work together as a whole class or in small groups to create new stanzas for the poem. Make sure that students follow the rhyme pattern. Students might also create a mural to illustrate the poem.

July

Crunch, munch,
Have some lunch!
Family picnic in the park.

Whizzle, fizzle,
Sparklers sizzle.
Write your name into the dark.

Tooting, hooting,
Flag saluting,
Big parade goes marching by!

Booming, zooming,
Colors blooming.
Fireworks light up the sky.

—Lana Krumwiede

Understanding the Poem

Read each question and choose the best answer. You may wish to reread "July" as you work.

1. In the poem, the family picnic is held _____.
Ⓐ in the backyard
Ⓑ at the beach
Ⓒ in the park
Ⓓ in the car

2. In the first stanza, the word **munch** means _____.
Ⓐ sing
Ⓑ eat
Ⓒ play
Ⓓ sleep

3. This poem is mainly about things that happen _____.
Ⓐ on the Fourth of July
Ⓑ on Halloween
Ⓒ in the winter
Ⓓ every day

4. The author of this poem probably _____.
Ⓐ has never seen a parade
Ⓑ has never seen fireworks
Ⓒ does not like going to the park
Ⓓ enjoys the Fourth of July holiday

5. You can tell from the last stanza that fireworks are _____.
Ⓐ smoky
Ⓑ boring
Ⓒ noisy and colorful
Ⓓ big and expensive

Understanding the Poem

1. What is a picnic? Write your answer in a complete sentence.

_____

_____

2. Many words in this poem describe sounds. List three of these sound words.

_____ _____ _____

3. Close your eyes and listen to the sounds around you. Write three words that describe the sounds you hear.

_____ _____ _____

4. List some of the things you might see in a parade. Use your imagination.

_____

_____

5. Draw a picture of a scene from the poem. Give your picture a title or label the people and things in your scene.

_____

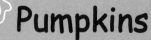

Before You Read the Poem

Build Background

Tell students that the history of the jack-o'-lantern can be traced back to an Irish legend about an unsavory character named Stingy Jack. Because of his disagreeable character, Stingy Jack wandered the Earth with only a lantern to guide his way. He became known as "Jack of the Lantern," which was soon shortened to "Jack O'Lantern."

Brainstorm Autumn Traditions

Carving pumpkins into jack-o'-lanterns is just one autumn custom. Ask students to work in pairs to brainstorm other autumn activities. If necessary, help them get started by brainstorming one or two activities as a whole class before students break into pairs. Examples might include picking apples, going for hayrides, trick-or-treating, visiting pumpkin patches, telling spooky stories, and watching scary movies.

While You Read the Poem

Ask students to read the poem one or two times silently in preparation for a choral reading. Because the word *pumpkins* is repeated often, the poem lends itself to a group reading; the result is almost a sing-along. Have the class read the poem aloud together two or three times.

After You Read the Poem

Elements of Poetry

Form: Rhyming Couplets Ask a student volunteer to point out rhyming words in the poem. Guide class discussion toward an understanding of rhyme as a literary device in which the last word in two different lines ends with the same vowel and ending sound. Help students see that poets use rhyme to help spoken words sound musical. You might even note that popular music, especially rap, relies heavily on rhyme. Remind students that a couplet is two consecutive lines of rhyming verse. Find examples in the poem.

Poet's Toolbox: Repetition Direct students' attention to the repetition used in the poem. The poet repeats the word *pumpkins* in every line except the last. Because the word is used repeatedly, the poem evokes the feeling of being surrounded by a multitude of pumpkins of all shapes and sizes. The last line of the poem lets us know that the speaker has a decision to make. Of all the pumpkins, she or he can select only one.

Follow-up Activities

Students may work independently to complete the activities on pages 42 and 43.

Pumpkins

Pumpkins oval, pumpkins round,
Pumpkins tumbling on the ground;
Pumpkins giant, pumpkins small,
Pumpkins lined against the wall;
Pumpkins squat and pumpkins high,
Pumpkins piled to the sky.
Pumpkins orange, pumpkins gold;
Pumpkins even white, I'm told.
Pumpkins fat and pumpkins thin,
Pumpkins with rough, bumpy skin.
Pumpkins pretty, pumpkins fun;
Oh, how can I pick just one?

—*Virginia Kroll*

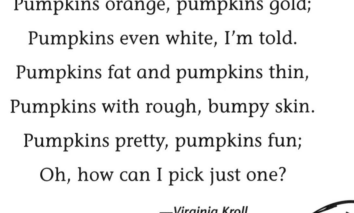

Name _____

Pumpkins

Understanding the Poem

Read each question and choose the best answer. You may wish to reread "Pumpkins" as you work.

1. Which of the following is <u>not</u> used in the poem as a color of pumpkins?

Ⓐ orange

Ⓑ purple

Ⓒ white

Ⓓ gold

2. Which of the following word pairs does <u>not</u> rhyme?

Ⓐ high, sky

Ⓑ thin, skin

Ⓒ small, wall

Ⓓ right, wrong

3. During which season do you think this poem takes place?

Ⓐ winter

Ⓑ spring

Ⓒ autumn

Ⓓ summer

4. What must the speaker in this poem do?

Ⓐ select a pumpkin

Ⓑ plant pumpkin seeds

Ⓒ visit a pumpkin patch

Ⓓ make a jack-o'-lantern

5. Which of the following words is <u>not</u> used in the poem to describe pumpkins?

Ⓐ fat

Ⓑ scary

Ⓒ small

Ⓓ round

Read and Understand Poetry • EMC 3323 • ©2005 by Evan-Moor Corp.

Pumpkins

Understanding the Poem

1. Look at the different kinds of pumpkins below. Draw a different jack-o'-lantern face to go with each one. Then write a label that describes each pumpkin, such as "silly pumpkin."

_____   _____   _____   _____

_____   _____   _____   _____

2. Complete the poem below by filling in the blanks with a rhyming word from the box. The first one has been done for you.

more	fun	about	night

At Halloween the spooks are out,

Bats and broomsticks fly ____**about**____.

Costumed kids go door to door

Collecting candy, treats, and _____.

A haunted house, a creepy sight,

Scares the children through the _____.

The ghouls that make you scream and run

Also make Halloween _____!

Before You Read the Poem

Build Background

Tell students that evergreens have been a symbol of renewed life since ancient times; help them see that this is because these trees stay green throughout the year. In many ancient cultures, people brought living greenery into the home at the time of the winter solstice—the longest night of the year. By the 1400s and 1500s, people in some parts of Europe set up decorated fir trees in their homes at Christmastime. By the 1800s, the tradition had spread through Europe and to the Americas. The first national Christmas tree in the United States was lighted in 1923 on the White House lawn by President Calvin Coolidge.

While You Read the Poem

As you read the poem aloud, ask students to try to picture each scene. Pause briefly after each stanza to allow students to process the images. You may wish to distribute drawing paper and crayons so that children may draw what their mind's eye sees.

After You Read the Poem

Elements of Poetry

Form: Free Verse Explain that "little tree" is written as free verse; in other words, it has no meter or rhyme. Because free verse does not have the usual conventions of poetry, many children have difficulty differentiating it from prose. Ask students to describe the images that are present in the poem: a small tree in a forest; a child hugging the tree; the tree's branches described as "arms" that hold the bright and shiny decorations; the decorated tree in the window; the two children dancing and singing around the tree. Explain that, unlike much prose, free verse often uses imagery to express many ideas in just a few lines.

Poet's Toolbox: Capitalization Have students review the poem text and circle the only two words that begin with a capital letter *(Christmas, Noel)*. Encourage them to suggest why other words that are usually capitalized, such as *I*, are not. Tell students that E. E. Cummings rarely used capital letters, and that the capitalization of *Christmas* and *Noel* are unusual for him. Students may wish to speculate about why the poet decided to capitalize these words.

Follow-up Activities

Students may work independently to complete the activities on pages 46 and 47.

Invite students to learn more about winter celebrations such as Hanukkah, Kwanzaa, Diwale, Winter Solstice, and others. They might begin at the following Web site: http://www.kidsdomain.com.

little tree

little tree
little silent Christmas tree
you are so little
you are more like a flower

who found you in the green forest
and were you very sorry to come away?
see   i will comfort you
because you smell so sweetly

i will kiss your cool bark
and hug you safe and tight
just as your mother would,
only don't be afraid

look   the spangles
that sleep all the year in a dark box
dreaming of being taken out and allowed to shine,
the balls the chains red and gold the fluffy threads,

put up your little arms
and i'll give them all to you to hold
every finger shall have its ring
and there won't be a single place dark or unhappy

then when you're quite dressed
you'll stand in the window for everyone to see
and how they'll stare!
oh but you'll be very proud

and my little sister and i will take hands
and looking up at our beautiful tree
we'll dance and sing
"Noel Noel"

—E. E. Cummings

Understanding the Poem

Read each question and choose the best answer. You may wish to reread "little tree" as you work.

1. Who is the "i" in the poem?
- Ⓐ the tree
- Ⓑ the poet
- Ⓒ the narrator
- Ⓓ the tree's mother

2. In this poem, the word **spangles** means _____.
- Ⓐ earrings
- Ⓑ bracelets
- Ⓒ artificial flowers
- Ⓓ tree decorations

3. The "little arms" in the poem are really _____.
- Ⓐ tree trunks
- Ⓑ tree branches
- Ⓒ the narrator's arms
- Ⓓ the little sister's arms

4. Who or what is the narrator talking to in this poem?
- Ⓐ a dog
- Ⓑ the tree
- Ⓒ a flower
- Ⓓ the little sister

5. What does "when you're quite dressed" mean?
- Ⓐ when the tree is decorated
- Ⓑ when the tree is in the forest
- Ⓒ when the sister sings "Noel Noel"
- Ⓓ when the narrator puts on his good clothes

Name _____

Understanding the Poem

1. The poem "little tree" contains many images of Christmas. Draw a picture of each scene below.

| 1. i will kiss your cool bark | 2. every finger shall have its ring |
| 3. you'll stand in the window for everyone to see | 4. we'll dance and sing "Noel, Noel" |

2. The narrator in the poem tells the little tree not to be afraid. Why might the tree be afraid?

_____

_____

3. The narrator says that he will dress up the tree with spangles. Circle the words in this list that could be "spangles" for the tree. Cross out the other words.

tinsel	lights	branches
pinecones	pine needles	coal
glass ornaments	a bright star	

Stuff & Nonsense

Contents

Before You Read the Poem

Build Background

This poem is a good example of nonsense verse, a genre characterized by humor and whimsy. Often, the author will invent new words to describe the characters and happenings in the poem. Edward Lear is one of the best-known writers of nonsense verse.

While You Read the Poem

Tell students that you are going to read them a fun and silly poem. Ask them to close their eyes, then simply sit back and enjoy the sounds of the words in the poem. After reading, ask students to recall some of the funny words they heard. Go through the poem together to find nonsense words such as *crumpetty, bibbons,* and *fimble.* Allow students to suggest meanings for the words.

After You Read the Poem

Elements of Poetry

Form: Couplets Remind students that couplets are sets of two rhyming lines. Assign a stanza to partners and ask them to find the couplet in it. Remind them that three rhyming lines are not a couplet; a couplet is only two lines that rhyme. Have partners share their findings with the group. Help students notice the pattern that should become apparent as they present their findings.

Poet's Toolbox: Rhythm Lear utilizes powerful rhythms that give this poem an almost musical feel. After a few readings, encourage children to stand and silently "dance" or move to the poem's rhythm as you read.

Follow-up Activities

Students may work independently to complete the activities on pages 52 and 53.

The Quangle Wangle's Hat

On the top of the Crumpetty Tree
    The Quangle Wangle sat,
But his face you could not see,
    On account of his Beaver Hat.
For his Hat was a hundred and two feet wide,
With ribbons and bibbons on every side
And bells, and buttons, and loops, and lace,
So that nobody ever could see the face
    Of the Quangle Wangle Quee.

The Quangle Wangle said
    To himself on the Crumpetty Tree,—
"Jam; and jelly; and bread;
    Are the best of food for me!
But the longer I live on the Crumpetty Tree
The plainer than ever it seems to me
That very few people come this way
And that life on the whole is far from gay!"
    Said the Quangle Wangle Quee.

But there came to the Crumpetty Tree,
    Mr. and Mrs. Canary;
And they said,—"Did you ever see
    Any spot so charmingly airy?
May we build a nest on your lovely Hat?
Mr. Quangle Wangle, grant us that!
O please let us come and build a nest
Of whatever material suits you best,
    Mr. Quangle Wangle Quee!"

Read and Understand Poetry • EMC 3323 • ©2005 by Evan-Moor Corp.

And besides, to the Crumpetty Tree
  Came the Stork, the Duck, and the Owl;
The Snail, and the Bumble-Bee,
  The Frog, and the Fimble Fowl;
(The Fimble Fowl, with a corkscrew leg;)
And all of them said,—"We humbly beg,
We may build our homes on your lovely Hat,—
Mr. Quangle Wangle, grant us that!
  Mr. Quangle Wangle Quee!"

And the Golden Grouse came there,
  And the Pobble who has no toes,—
And the small Olympian bear,—
  And the Dong with a luminous nose.
And the Blue Baboon, who played the Flute,—
And the Orient Calf from the Land of Tute,—
And the Attery Squash, and Bisky Bat,—
All came and built on the lovely Hat
  Of the Quangle Wangle Quee.

And the Quangle Wangle said
  To himself on the Crumpetty Tree,—
"When all these creatures move
  What a wonderful noise there'll be!"
And at night by the light of the Mulberry moon
They danced to the Flute of the Blue Baboon,
On the broad green leaves of the Crumpetty Tree,
And all were as happy as happy could be,
  With the Quangle Wangle Quee.

—Edward Lear

Stuff & Nonsense

Understanding the Poem

Read each question and choose the best answer. You may wish to reread "The Quangle Wangle's Hat" as you work.

1. What does the Quangle Wangle like to eat?
  Ⓐ jam and jelly and bread
  Ⓑ peanuts and popcorn
  Ⓒ apples and bananas
  Ⓓ pie and cookies

2. Who comes to the Crumpetty Tree first?
  Ⓐ Bisky Bat
  Ⓑ the Pobble
  Ⓒ the Blue Baboon
  Ⓓ Mr. and Mrs. Canary

3. All the creatures want to build their homes on the Quangle Wangle's _____.
  Ⓐ back
  Ⓑ hat
  Ⓒ shoe
  Ⓓ nose

4. How did the Quangle Wangle feel about all the creatures moving in?
  Ⓐ mad
  Ⓑ tired
  Ⓒ happy
  Ⓓ afraid

5. Which item is <u>not</u> one of the decorations on the Quangle Wangle's hat?
  Ⓐ lace
  Ⓑ bells
  Ⓒ buttons
  Ⓓ balloons

Read and Understand Poetry • EMC 3323 • ©2005 by Evan-Moor Corp.

Understanding the Poem

1. Draw a picture of each of these imaginary creatures.

Pobble	**Fimble Fowl**
Attery Squash	**Bisky Bat**

2. Write a story about one or more of the creatures. Use at least one nonsense word in your story. Of course, this will be a nonsense story!

_____

_____

_____

_____

_____

_____

_____

Before You Read the Poems

Build Background

The limerick is a form of poetry that was hugely popular in the late nineteenth and early twentieth centuries. Edward Lear is the most famous author of limericks. His *Book of Nonsense* was published in 1846 and is still enjoyed today.

Build Vocabulary

Encourage students to give the meaning for words on this list that are familiar; provide simple definitions for unfamiliar words.

bonnet: a woman's hat

habit: a usual or regular practice or behavior

induced: to be forced or made to do something

relinquished: gave up

unique: one of a kind

While You Read the Poems

Ask students to read along silently as you read each limerick. Then read the limericks again, asking students to chime in on the rhyming words. Finally, ask students to take turns reading the limericks aloud.

After You Read the Poems

Elements of Poetry

Form: Limerick Limericks are characterized by a very specific form and rhyme scheme. Help students identify these characteristics of limericks:

- Each limerick has five lines.

- The rhyme scheme is *aabba* (i.e., the first, second, and fifth lines rhyme, and the third and fourth lines rhyme).

Poet's Toolbox: Hyperbole Most limericks are intended to be funny. One tool that writers use to add humor in limericks is hyperbole. Explain to students that extreme exaggeration is called *hyperbole*. Ask students to find some examples of hyperbole in the limericks they have just read. (Examples: "All the birds of the air" could not possibly fit on a bonnet. No one could really eat 18 rabbits.)

Follow-up Activities

Students may work independently to complete the activities on pages 56 and 57.

1

There was a young lady whose bonnet
Came untied when the birds sat upon it.
But she said, "I don't care!
All the birds of the air
Are welcome to sit on my bonnet!"

2

There was an old person whose habits
Induced him to feed upon rabbits.
When he'd eaten eighteen
He turned perfectly green
Upon which he relinquished those habits.

3

There was a young lady whose eyes
Were unique as to color and size.
When she opened them wide
People all turned aside
And started away in surprise.

—Edward Lear

Understanding the Poems

Read each question and choose the best answer. You may wish to reread the limericks as you work.

1. What color did the "old person" in limerick 2 turn?

- Ⓐ blue
- Ⓑ pink
- Ⓒ green
- Ⓓ orange

2. In limerick 1, why did the young lady's bonnet come untied?

- Ⓐ A dog sat on it.
- Ⓑ The birds sat on it.
- Ⓒ The wind was blowing.
- Ⓓ The birds flew away with it.

3. What does the phrase "feed upon" mean?

- Ⓐ eat
- Ⓑ sell
- Ⓒ talk to
- Ⓓ give food to

4. In limerick 3, you can tell that the young lady's eyes are _____.

- Ⓐ normal
- Ⓑ deep blue
- Ⓒ dark brown
- Ⓓ very strange

5. How does the "young lady" in limerick 1 probably feel about birds?

- Ⓐ She does not like birds.
- Ⓑ She likes birds very much.
- Ⓒ She wants all the birds to go away.
- Ⓓ She does not want the birds to ruin her hat.

Understanding the Poems

1. Draw a picture to illustrate one of the limericks. Write the number of the limerick.

2. Fill in the blanks to complete a new limerick.

There once was a monkey named Jed

Who jumped up and down on the _____.

He fell down with a thump

And got up with a _____

On the top of his hard little _____.

3. Create a limerick of your own.

_____

_____

_____

_____

_____

Before You Read the Poem

Build Background

Ask students to consider their bedtime routine. Do they have a set bedtime? Do they read or do other relaxing activities before falling asleep? How many hours of sleep do they tend to get each night? Tell them that the National Sleep Foundation recommends that children between the ages of five and twelve should get nine to eleven hours of sleep every night. Lack of sleep may make it more difficult to do well at school and can even contribute to more childhood injuries! Tell students that they are going to read a poem written from the point of view of a child who is extremely tired.

While You Read the Poem

Ask students to pretend they are very, very sleepy. They may wish to stretch, yawn, put their head on their desk, or make snoring sounds. Invite them to imagine how it would feel to have to walk upstairs when feeling so sleepy. Then ask a volunteer to read the poem aloud in a sleepy voice, replete with yawns and heavy sighs.

After You Read the Poem

Elements of Poetry

Form: Concrete Poem Ask students to comment on the poem's form and structure. Be sure to note that the poem is unusual because it is read from bottom to top rather than from top to bottom. Help students see that the lines of the poem resemble the stairs that the poem's narrator must climb in order to get to bed. Poems in which the shape or design contributes to the overall meaning are called *concrete poems* or *shape poems*.

Poet's Toolbox: Rhyme Only two rhyming words are found in this poem *(steep and asleep)*. Ask students to offer possible reasons why the poet included these words (e.g., to stress the difficulty of the climb and the desired outcome of sleep; to mark the middle and end of the poem; to make the poem sound melodic). Remind students that rhyme is a common tool in a poet's toolbox.

Poet's Toolbox: Repetition In this poem, the word *so* is repeated *(so so)* each time it is used. Guide students to the understanding that in this case, the poet uses repetition to help stress just how tired the narrator is and just how steep the stairs are. Ask students how the poem would be different if the poet had written "I'm very tired" or "These stairs are very steep." If necessary, point out that *so so* adds to the feeling of exhaustion expressed in the poem.

Follow-up Activities

Students may work independently to complete the activities on pages 60 and 61.

Up the Stairs to Bed

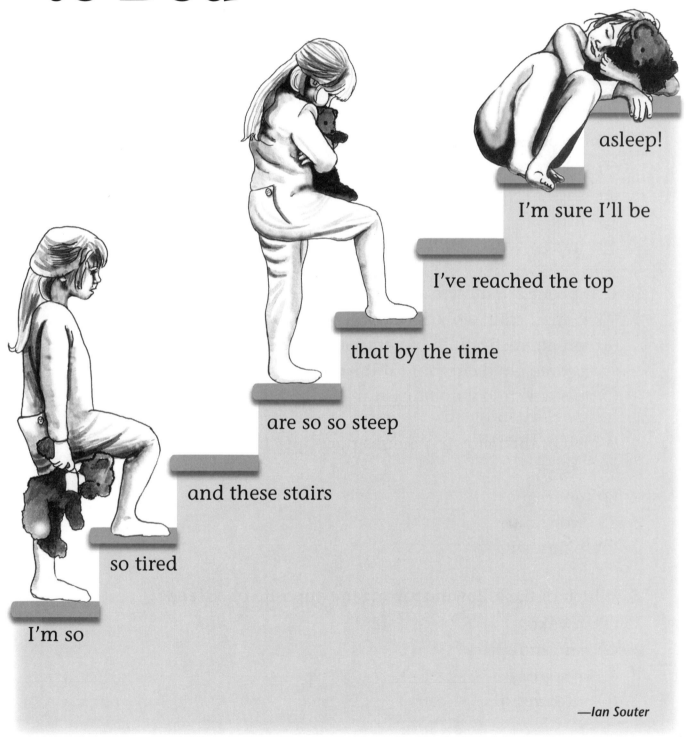

asleep!

I'm sure I'll be

I've reached the top

that by the time

are so so steep

and these stairs

so tired

I'm so

—Ian Souter

Up the Stairs to Bed

Understanding the Poem

Read each question and choose the best answer. You may wish to reread "Up the Stairs to Bed" as you work.

1. In the poem, a child is feeling _____ .

   Ⓐ happy

   Ⓑ excited

   Ⓒ sleepy

   Ⓓ upset

2. Which of these is another word for **steep**?

   Ⓐ small

   Ⓑ short

   Ⓒ little

   Ⓓ high

3. This poem is mainly about _____ .

   Ⓐ a tired child walking down the stairs

   Ⓑ an energetic child playing out-of-doors

   Ⓒ a tired child climbing stairs on the way to bed

   Ⓓ a tired child who must stay awake for several more hours

4. Which of the following means the opposite of **tired**?

   Ⓐ sleepy

   Ⓑ energetic

   Ⓒ worn out

   Ⓓ exhausted

5. Which of the following means the opposite of **asleep**?

   Ⓐ awake

   Ⓑ snoring

   Ⓒ napping

   Ⓓ dreaming

 Read and Understand Poetry • EMC 3323 • ©2005 by Evan-Moor Corp.

Understanding the Poem

1. The poet uses rhyming words in this poem. Write at least three more words that rhyme with **steep** and **asleep**. One way to make rhyming words is to replace the first letter of a word with other letters of the alphabet.

   _____

   _____

2. "Up the Stairs to Bed" is called a **concrete**, or **shape** poem because the shape made by the words of the poem adds to its meaning. Write your own poems using the shapes below. The first one has been done for you.

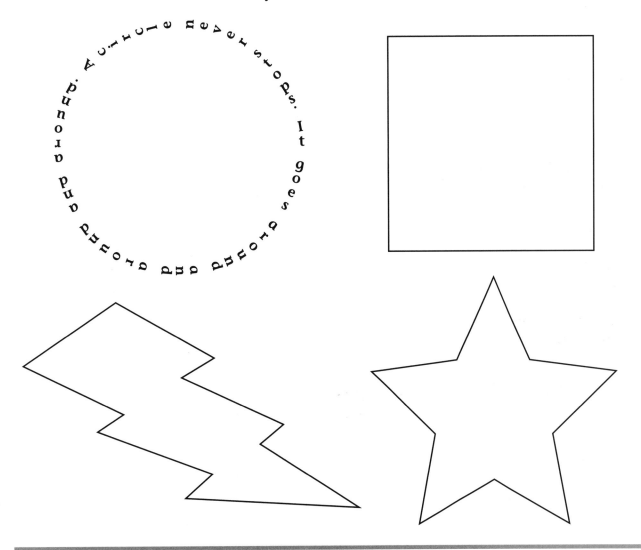

Before You Read the Poem

Build Background

Tell students that they are going to read a poem by Henry Wadsworth Longfellow. Longfellow was born almost 200 years ago and is one of America's most beloved poets. The poet wrote "There Was a Little Girl" for his baby daughter. He sang the lines to her as he carried her in his arms.

Build Vocabulary

Remind students that Longfellow wrote his poems many years ago. The English language has changed some since that time. Many new and different words are used now that were unfamiliar to Longfellow, such as *computer* and *cell phone*. Point out that in the same way, some of the words used in Longfellow's time are not so common now. Invite students to conjecture about the meaning of *horrid*, one of the words used by Longfellow in this poem. Encourage them to say what it's like when someone or something is horrid. Make sure they know that it means "terrible."

While You Read the Poem

Have students read through "There Was a Little Girl" silently. Then read the poem aloud for them, emphasizing its rhythmic nature. Invite children to stand and move to the rhythm of the poem, imagining they are holding a fussy baby who needs to be calmed. Other volunteers may wish to read or recite for the group.

After You Read the Poem

Elements of Poetry

Poet's Toolbox: Rhyme Remind students that poets use rhyming words to help make their writing less like a story and more like a song. Work with students to find the words that rhyme in this poem. They will get more practice with this on the second activity page.

Poet's Toolbox: Rhythm Tell students that the rhythm of a poem can be felt both in its words and in the pauses that come between them. Recite the poem for the children, emphasizing the pause after *forehead* and the sense of finality after *horrid*. Invite students to clap or tap a steady beat and to recite the poem, noting how some of the words fall right on the beat, adding weight or emphasis to them.

Follow-up Activities

Students may work independently to complete the activities on pages 64 and 65.

There Was a Little Girl

There was a little girl,
Who had a little curl,
Right in the middle
of her forehead.
When she was good,
She was very good indeed,
But when she was bad
she was horrid.

—Henry Wadsworth Longfellow

Understanding the Poem

Read each question and choose the best answer. You may wish to reread "There Was a Little Girl" as you work.

1. Where was the little girl's curl?
- Ⓐ on the top of her head
- Ⓑ down by her shoulders
- Ⓒ on the right side of her head
- Ⓓ in the center of her forehead

2. From this poem, you can tell that the little girl _____.
- Ⓐ is never good
- Ⓑ has messy hair
- Ⓒ is well-behaved sometimes
- Ⓓ likes to be carried and rocked

3. What might the little girl do when she acts horrid?
- Ⓐ take a nap
- Ⓑ scream and cry
- Ⓒ clean up her toys
- Ⓓ eat all her vegetables

4. How does the narrator probably feel about the little girl?
- Ⓐ He doesn't like her curl.
- Ⓑ He really doesn't care for her.
- Ⓒ He is scared by the way she acts.
- Ⓓ He knows she can't always be good.

5. Which word does <u>not</u> mean the same as **horrid**?
- Ⓐ awful
- Ⓑ terrible
- Ⓒ wonderful
- Ⓓ impossible

   Read and Understand Poetry • EMC 3323 • ©2005 by Evan-Moor Corp.

Understanding the Poem

1. Not all words that rhyme are spelled the same way. Read this list of words. Put the words that rhyme in the same group. Look at the way they are spelled.

girl	right	pearl	wood	light	good
bite	should	white	curl	whirl	could

_____   _____   _____

_____   _____   _____

_____   _____   _____

_____   _____   _____

2. How might a horrid little girl act? List some things she might do.

_____

_____

3. Draw a picture of the little girl with the curl. Is she being good or horrid? Write a sentence that tells what she is doing.

_____

_____

Step Outside

Contents

Before You Read the Poem

Build Background

Invite students to talk about the experience of swinging on a swing. Ask them to describe how it feels and what they like (or dislike) about it. Tell students that they will be reading another poem by Robert Louis Stevenson from his collection *A Child's Garden of Verses*. Remind them that they also read "Bed in Summer" from the same collection.

While You Read the Poem

Ask students to read the poem silently. Then read the poem aloud while they follow along. Encourage volunteers to read the poem aloud. Can they feel the motion of the swing?

After You Read the Poem

Elements of Poetry

Poet's Toolbox: Rhyme Scheme In each four-line verse, the first and third lines end with words that rhyme, and the second and fourth lines end with words that rhyme. Guide students in marking this *abab* rhyme scheme by writing one of these letters at the end of each line. Ask volunteers to say the words that rhyme in the lines marked with the same letter.

Poet's Toolbox: Hyperbole Remind students that *hyperbole* is intentional use of exaggeration. There are several examples in this poem: the narrator declares that swinging is not just pleasant, but in fact the pleasantest thing that a child can do; he says he can swing high enough to see the whole countryside; he compares swinging to flying. Help students understand how these are examples of exaggeration and discuss them.

Follow-up Activities

Students may work independently to complete the activities on pages 69 and 70.

The Swing

How do you like to go up in a swing,
Up in the air so blue?
Oh, I do think it the pleasantest thing
Ever a child can do!

Up in the air and over the wall,
Till I can see so wide,
River and trees and cattle and all
Over the countryside—

Till I look down on the garden green,
Down on the roof so brown—
Up in the air I go flying again,
Up in the air and down!

—Robert Louis Stevenson

Understanding the Poem

Read each question and choose the best answer. You may wish to reread "The Swing" as you work.

1. From the swing, the child sees _____.

   Ⓐ a river, trees, and cattle

   Ⓑ a pond, hills, and horses

   Ⓒ a lake, mountains, and snow

   Ⓓ the ocean, beach, and boats

2. This poem is mainly about the joy of _____.

   Ⓐ being alone

   Ⓑ going to school

   Ⓒ playing on a swing

   Ⓓ living in the country

3. The word **pleasantest** means the most _____.

   Ⓐ tiring

   Ⓑ scary

   Ⓒ boring

   Ⓓ enjoyable

4. Which color word appears first in the poem?

   Ⓐ red

   Ⓑ blue

   Ⓒ green

   Ⓓ yellow

5. The action in the poem takes place _____.

   Ⓐ in the city

   Ⓑ on a boat

   Ⓒ on a train

   Ⓓ in the country

Name _____

The Swing

Understanding the Poem

1. How does the narrator in this poem feel about playing on a swing?

_____

_____

2. Write the three color words that appear in the poem.

_____   _____   _____

Think of three more words that describe colors. Write them below.

_____   _____   _____

3. Find a word in the poem that rhymes with each of these words. Then add two more rhyming words to each list.

wall	**brown**	**wide**	**blue**
_____	_____	_____	_____
_____	_____	_____	_____
_____	_____	_____	_____

4. Imagine that you are on a swing near your home or school. What colors and things would you see as you fly high in the air? What sounds would you hear? Write your ideas on this chart.

Colors	Things	Sounds

Read and Understand Poetry • EMC 3323 • ©2005 by Evan-Moor Corp.

Before You Read the Poem

Build Background

Ask students to share what they already know about fog. For example, they might say that it's hard to see in the fog or that fog is wet. Be sure to mention that fog is actually a collection of water or ice droplets close to the ground. Fog is really a cloud that is close to the surface of the Earth. It forms when moisture collects on dust particles in the air. Among other causes, fog can form when warm water evaporates into cool air, when warm rain falls through cool air, or when heat rises from the ground during a cool night.

While You Read the Poem

Ask a volunteer to read the poem aloud, trying to read smoothly from beginning to end without pausing. Invite the whole class to read the poem chorally. Remind students not to make much of a pause at the end of the first two lines.

After You Read the Poem

Elements of Poetry

Poet's Toolbox: Punctuation Ask students to identify the only punctuation mark in the poem (the final period). Ask students why they think there is no period at the end of lines one and two. They may remember that poetry does not always use punctuation. In this case, however, point out that this poem is actually one long sentence that has been broken up into three lines. That is why the period appears at the very end.

Poet's Toolbox: Simile Explain to students that a *simile* compares one thing to another by using the word *like* or *as*. Ask students to identify the two things being compared ("lines of cars" and "mechanical caterpillar"). Invite a volunteer to use pantomime, or gestures, to show how a caterpillar pulls its body together, then stretches out again to move. Have students look at the illustration of the cars going over the hilly road to see how the cars "rising and dipping with the humps of the road" might look like a caterpillar.

Follow-up Activities

Students may work independently to complete the activities on pages 73 and 74.

Fog

Lines of cars inch along in the fog
Rising and dipping with the humps of the road
Like a mechanical caterpillar.

—*Nancy R. Wadhams*

Understanding the Poem

Read each question and choose the best answer. You may wish to reread "Fog" as you work.

1. In the poem, cars are probably moving slowly because _____.
- Ⓐ the fog makes it hard for drivers to see
- Ⓑ a red traffic light is telling them to stop
- Ⓒ people are crossing the street
- Ⓓ there is a traffic jam

2. In the poem, what does the word **inch** mean?
- Ⓐ a measurement on a ruler
- Ⓑ move along slowly
- Ⓒ stop suddenly
- Ⓓ run quickly

3. This poem is mainly about _____.
- Ⓐ how mechanical things look alike
- Ⓑ the humps on the back of a caterpillar
- Ⓒ the way caterpillars move on a foggy day
- Ⓓ how cars in the fog look like a slow-moving caterpillar

4. In the poem, which of these means the opposite of **rising**?
- Ⓐ increasing
- Ⓑ growing
- Ⓒ dipping
- Ⓓ inching

5. Which of these is most like a caterpillar?
- Ⓐ an inchworm
- Ⓑ a butterfly
- Ⓒ a cocoon
- Ⓓ an ant

Understanding the Poem

1. The poem "Fog" compares a line of cars to a caterpillar. When a comparison uses the word **like** or **as**, it is called a **simile**. Use the words in the box to complete the following similes.

| lion | balloon | clown | cheetah | stars |

The runner was as fast as a _____ .

My best friend is as funny as a _____ .

My coach is as strong as a _____ .

The sun is like a yellow _____ .

The lights on the cars were like _____ .

2. Fill in the blanks to complete your own poem.

On snowy mornings,

I move as quickly as a _____ .

Down the stairs,

as swift as a _____ .

Out the door,

as fast as a _____ .

Into the snow,

I dive like a _____ .

I make snow angels

and snowmen

and snow forts.

On snowy mornings,

I move as quickly as a _____ .

3. Draw a picture on the back of this page to illustrate your poem.

Before You Read the Poem

Build Background

Tell students that they are about to read a poem about something they find at a playground. Invite several volunteers to guess what the poem might be about. Then work with the group to brainstorm a list of words that name their actions when they are playing at a park or playground, such as *run, jump,* and *swing.* After you review the list, tell students that they are going to read a poem that illustrates, with words, one of those actions: sliding.

While You Read the Poem

Have students take turns reading the poem to a partner. Invite volunteers to say what they notice about the way the poem is written, with the words themselves forming the shape of a slide, which is the subject of the poem. Tell students that poems whose shape adds more meaning to the poem are called *shape poems.* Another name for shape poems is *concrete poems.*

After You Read the Poem

Elements of Poetry

Form: Concrete Poem Ask students to speculate about why poets might use the shape of a poem to communicate meaning. Guide them in an understanding of how design and words combine to create a total visual effect. In essence, the shape made by the words themselves illustrates the meaning of the poem; it contributes to the feelings the poem evokes.

Poet's Toolbox: Diction and Alliteration Poets often choose specific words to communicate precise meaning. In this poem, the poet uses short, choppy words to show the step-by-step climb up the slide. At the top, the poet uses alliteration (the repetition of the beginning consonant sound in words that are close together in the poem, such as *slick slide*) to reflect the rapid movement down the slide. The poet also uses alliteration to signal a quick stop: *feet first flop!*

Follow-up Activities

Students may work independently to complete the activities on pages 77 and 78.

top

the

to

one

by

one

steps

the

Up

slick slide down again feet first flop!

—Beverly McLoughland

Concrete Poem

Understanding the Poem

Read each question and choose the best answer. You may wish to reread the concrete poem as you work.

1. What is the subject of this poem?
- Ⓐ a jungle gym
- Ⓑ a swing set
- Ⓒ a seesaw
- Ⓓ a slide

2. Which of these word pairs is an example of alliteration?
- Ⓐ one by
- Ⓑ the steps
- Ⓒ slick slide
- Ⓓ down again

3. Which of the following best describes what this poem is about?
- Ⓐ playing on a slide
- Ⓑ having fun at school
- Ⓒ slipping and falling down
- Ⓓ getting tired from climbing

4. "Feet first flop!" is an example of _____ .
- Ⓐ haiku
- Ⓑ rhyme
- Ⓒ syllables
- Ⓓ alliteration

5. Which word means about the same as **slick**?
- Ⓐ small
- Ⓑ sticky
- Ⓒ slippery
- Ⓓ surprising

Concrete Poem

Understanding the Poem

Write words on the shapes below to create your own shape poems.
Try to choose words that say something about the shape.
Use the example for ideas.

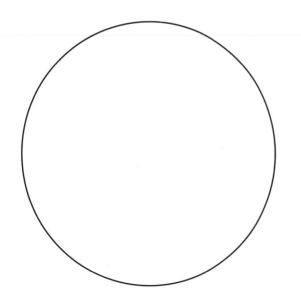

Before You Read the Poem

Build Background

Tell students that the poem they will read next is called "The Pasture." Ask students if they know what a pasture is. You may need to explain that a pasture is a field where grass and other plants grow. Sometimes cows or other animals eat grass, or graze, in a pasture. Invite volunteers to say what a spring found in a pasture might be. Make sure they know that a spring is a place where water comes out of the ground and forms a pool. Encourage students to deduce why having a spring in a pasture could be a good thing (grazing animals can drink there). Invite students to close their eyes and make a picture in their mind of a calf in a pasture. Have volunteers describe their images for the group. Use prompts to elicit more details: *Is the calf's mother nearby? Is the calf standing up? Is it wobbly or steady?*

Build Vocabulary

Remind students that contractions are two separate words that have been put together to make one word. An apostrophe is placed in the spot where one or more letters were taken out of the words. Encourage students to provide some examples, such as *I'm* or *can't*. Then write *sha'n't* on the chalkboard and invite students to speculate on the two words used to form this contraction. Show them how *shall not* has been contracted into this word—an old-fashioned way of saying *shall not*, which means the same thing as *will not* or the contraction *won't*.

While You Read the Poem

Ask students to read along silently as you read the poem aloud. Check to make sure that students understand the meaning of *fetch* and *totters* within the context of the poem. Then invite volunteers to take turns reading the poem aloud, with each reading one stanza.

After You Read the Poem

Elements of Poetry

Poet's Toolbox: Run-on Lines Ask students to look at the punctuation at the end of each line of the poem. Some lines end in periods, which we use to end a sentence. But some lines "run" into the next line. Write the first three lines of the second stanza on the chalkboard or other display as if they were prose sentences, not poetry. Ask students to read the sentences aloud. Then ask a volunteer to try to read the poem the same way, pausing only where the poet used a period, semicolon, or comma.

Students may be interested in knowing that the formal name given to the use of "run-on" lines is *enjambement,* which contains the French word *jambe,* meaning "leg" (which is also used to "run on").

Follow-up Activities

Students may work independently to complete the activities on pages 81 and 82.

The Pasture

I'm going out to clean the pasture spring;
I'll only stop to rake the leaves away
(And wait to watch the water clear, I may):
I sha'n't be gone long.—You come too.

I'm going out to fetch the little calf
That's standing by the mother. It's so young,
It totters when she licks it with her tongue.
I sha'n't be gone long.—You come too.

—Robert Frost

Understanding the Poem

Read each question and choose the best answer. You may wish to reread "The Pasture" as you work.

1. Who is speaking in the poem?
- Ⓐ a calf
- Ⓑ a cow
- Ⓒ the pasture
- Ⓓ the narrator

2. What is the narrator going to do before cleaning the stream?
- Ⓐ fetch the calf
- Ⓑ wash his face
- Ⓒ rake out leaves
- Ⓓ clear away rocks

3. Where does the poem take place?
- Ⓐ by a lake in the woods
- Ⓑ in a large, grassy park
- Ⓒ on a farm in the country
- Ⓓ in a children's petting zoo

4. Which word means about the same as **totters**?
- Ⓐ cries
- Ⓑ sways
- Ⓒ crashes
- Ⓓ splashes

5. Why might a mother cow lick her calf?
- Ⓐ The cow is hungry.
- Ⓑ The calf needs washing.
- Ⓒ The cow's tongue is itchy.
- Ⓓ The calf asked her for a kiss.

The Pasture

Understanding the Poem

1. **Synonyms** are words that mean the same thing. Circle a synonym for each of the words below.

Word	Synonym		
spring	hinge	stream	faucet
pasture	field	woods	farm
fetch	feed	tease	get

2. "The Pasture" has several rhyming words. Circle the following pairs of words if they rhyme. If they do <u>not</u> rhyme, cross them out.

wait	watch	rake	away
gone	long	young	tongue
away	may	come	too

3. Draw a picture to go with "The Pasture." Be sure to include the spring, the calf, and the cow.

Read and Understand Poetry • EMC 3323 • ©2005 by Evan-Moor Corp.

Poems in Song

Contents

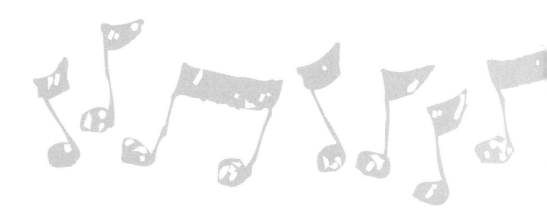

Before You Read the Poem

Build Background

Tell students that the next poem they will read, "Hush, Little Baby," is actually a traditional lullaby: a song used to help young children fall asleep. Students may be familiar with the song, and may even know different words. Explain that traditional songs are often hundreds of years old. People learn them by hearing them sung aloud and teach them to their children by singing the songs to them. That is why there are often many versions of traditional songs with small differences in the words they use. Invite children to share about lullabies or other traditional songs they have learned from parents or other family members.

While You Read the Poem

Read the poem while students follow along. Then have partners read the poem to each other. If you are familiar with the traditional melody, invite students to sing along with you. If not, you might learn the song at a Web site, such as http://www.singingbabies.com.

After You Read the Poem

Elements of Poetry

Poet's Toolbox: Repetition Point out repeated phrases: "If that . . ." and "Mama's gonna . . . ." Help students understand how this repetition produces a soothing, rhythmic effect. Remind students that the reason people sing lullabies is so children will calm down and go to sleep.

Poet's Toolbox: Variation Invite students to share any variations of this song that they know, or share some of these:

> "Papa's gonna" instead of "Mama's gonna"

> "a cart and mule" instead of "a cart and bull"

Invite students to speculate about how it's possible to end up with several versions of a traditional song and give other examples they know.

Follow-up Activities

Students may work independently to complete the activities on pages 86 and 87.

Hush, Little Baby

Hush, little baby, don't say a word.

Mama's gonna buy you a mockingbird.

If that mockingbird won't sing,

Mama's gonna buy you a diamond ring.

If that diamond ring turns brass,

Mama's gonna buy you a looking glass.

If that looking glass gets broke,

Mama's gonna buy you a billy goat.

If that billy goat won't pull,

Mama's gonna buy you a cart and bull.

If that cart and bull turn over,

Mama's gonna buy you a dog named Rover.

If that dog named Rover won't bark,

Mama's gonna buy you a horse and cart.

If that horse and cart break down,

You'll still be the sweetest little baby in town.

—**Traditional**

Hush, Little Baby

Understanding the Poem

Read each question and choose the best answer. You may wish to reread "Hush, Little Baby" as you work.

1. Which word rhymes with **sing** in "Hush, Little Baby"?

Ⓒ word

Ⓓ ring

Ⓔ diamond

Ⓕ mocking

2. What is the **looking glass**?

Ⓒ a pair of eyeglasses

Ⓓ a light bulb

Ⓔ a window

Ⓕ a mirror

3. Which of these items appears last in the poem?

Ⓒ a dog named Rover

Ⓓ a diamond ring

Ⓔ a horse and cart

Ⓕ a mockingbird

4. The word **cart** means _____.

Ⓒ a small wagon

Ⓓ a saddle

Ⓔ a crate

Ⓕ a car

5. The word **gonna** means _____.

Ⓒ gone

Ⓓ going to

Ⓔ not going to

Ⓕ hoping to

Read and Understand Poetry • EMC 3323 • ©2005 by Evan-Moor Corp.

Understanding the Poem

Create your own version of this lullaby. Try to follow the rhyme pattern of the traditional song. You may like to try working with a partner.

Hush, little baby, _____.

_____ gonna buy you a _____.

If that _____,

_____ gonna buy you a _____.

If that _____,

_____ gonna buy you a _____.

If that _____,

_____ gonna buy you a _____.

If that _____,

_____ gonna buy you a _____.

If that _____,

_____ gonna buy you a _____.

If that _____,

_____ gonna buy you a _____.

If that _____,

You'll still be the _____.

Share your song with a partner or the class.

Now, turn this page over and draw a picture to illustrate part of your song.

Before You Read the Poem

Build Background

Tell students that the next poem they will read, "Bright with Colors," is a traditional song that comes from Spanish-speaking countries. Some students may know "De colores," the original song in Spanish. Have students brainstorm where they might see bright colors in the spring. List their ideas, adding *flowers in fields, birds returning after winter,* and *rainbows* if they aren't listed. Discuss these elements and how they appear during the spring. You might explain how rainbows are formed during changeable spring weather when droplets of rain remain in the sky after sunlight breaks through the clouds. The light is split into beautiful colors as it passes through the raindrops. Tell students that a rainbow is just one example of the ways nature uses color to make our world more beautiful.

Listening to the Original

Invite a fluent Spanish-speaker to present the original song in Spanish. You might even host a parent or other guest to make a special presentation. Tell students that this song has been sung by people who work in the fields planting, tending, and harvesting the crops that give us food. People who work in agriculture are experienced in observing the fields and their changing colors.

While You Read the Poem

Read the English-language poem to the students, matching the rhythmic pattern to the Spanish-language original (if you know it). If you or any students know the traditional melody, try to sing it. Notice how the English words are able to fit in with the melody, just as the Spanish words do.

After You Read the Poem

Elements of Poetry

Form: Translation Point out the challenges of creating a version of a poem in another language. It is especially difficult to keep the rhythm and rhyme of the original in a translation. In this case, however, the translator did it! Read a line in English, such as "Bright with colors," then read the corresponding line in Spanish. Encourage all students to repeat the Spanish lines aloud.

Poet's Toolbox: Repetition Focus students on the repeating phrase "bright with colors." Together, count its occurrences in the poem (one per line in the first six lines). Have students speculate about why this phrase is repeated so often. Point out that repeating phrases add rhythm and make the words stand out more.

Follow-up Activities

Students may work independently to complete the activities on pages 90 and 91.

Bright with Colors

Bright with colors,
bright with colors are fields that dress themselves up in the spring.
Bright with colors,
bright with colors are all the small birds that fly in on the wing.
Bright with colors,
bright with colors the rainbow that you and I see when it shines.
And for all of these reasons the love of all colors
is something that I like just fine.
And for all of these reasons the love of all colors
is something that I like just fine.

—based on a traditional Mexican song; English version by Sarita Chávez Silverman

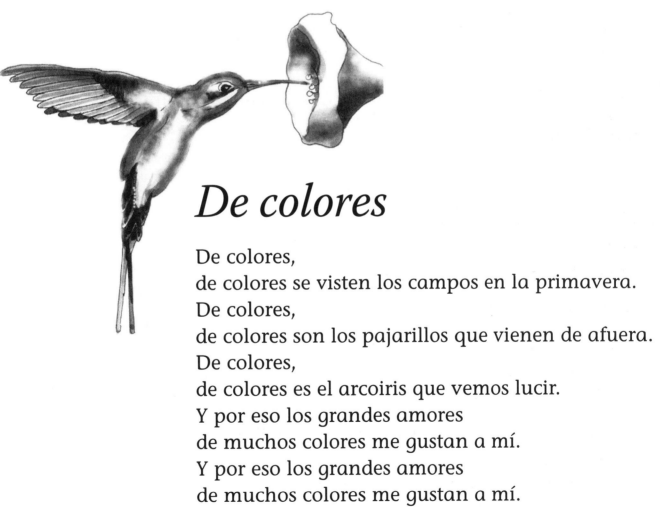

De colores

De colores,
de colores se visten los campos en la primavera.
De colores,
de colores son los pajarillos que vienen de afuera.
De colores,
de colores es el arcoiris que vemos lucir.
Y por eso los grandes amores
de muchos colores me gustan a mí.
Y por eso los grandes amores
de muchos colores me gustan a mí.

—canción tradicional mexicana

Understanding the Poem

Read each question and choose the best answer. You may wish to reread "Bright with Colors" as you work.

1. In this poem, which of these is something that is <u>not</u> bright with colors?

Ⓐ birds
Ⓑ fields
Ⓒ sunsets
Ⓓ rainbows

2. Which of these is a color?

Ⓐ dark
Ⓑ light
Ⓒ bright
Ⓓ green

3. How did the translator choose to say "de colores" in the poem in English?

Ⓐ I love colors
Ⓑ rainbow colors
Ⓒ birds with colors
Ⓓ bright with colors

4. When do the fields become colorful?

Ⓐ fall
Ⓑ spring
Ⓒ winter
Ⓓ summer

5. Which of these might be the type of bird in the poem?

Ⓐ a red bird
Ⓑ a gray bird
Ⓒ a white bird
Ⓓ a black bird

Bright with Colors

Understanding the Poem

1. This poem is about colors, but it doesn't mention any particular color. Write about your favorite color. Why do you like it best? Name some things you have that are your favorite color.

_____

_____

_____

2. The song says that the fields "dress themselves up in the spring" in bright colors. How do the fields dress up? Explain what this means.

_____

_____

_____

3. Read this list of things in nature. Which ones are also "bright with colors"? Circle them.

sand	a slug	a sunrise
a sunflower	a boulder	snow
a hummingbird	fire	grass

4. Draw a picture that shows the scene described in "Bright with Colors."

Before You Read the Poem

Build Background

The author of this poem, Sarah Josepha Hale, was born in 1788 and grew up on a farm. This poem is based on a childhood memory. Although Hale is best known for "Mary's Lamb," she led a very active and productive life. She was a teacher, a writer, and an editor of some of the leading magazines of her day. She also led the campaign to have Thanksgiving Day set aside as a national holiday.

Build Vocabulary

Encourage students to give the meaning for the words on this list that are familiar; provide simple definitions for any unfamiliar words:

bind: tie, connect

confidence: certainty

fleece: the wool of a sheep

lamb: a baby sheep

linger: stay, remain

patiently: without complaining

shield: protect

While You Read the Poem

The first verse of this poem is probably familiar to many students. Ask students to read the poem silently as you read it aloud.

Have volunteers play the roles of Mary, the lamb, the teacher, and the children. Ask them to pantomime the actions of these characters as the rest of the class reads the poem in unison.

After You Read the Poem

Elements of Poetry

Poet's Toolbox: Rhyme Scheme The general rhyme scheme of this poem is *ababcdcd*. Assist students in locating the rhyming words that support this rhyme scheme. Encourage them to find the lines in the first verse that do not follow this rhyme scheme.

Poet's Toolbox: Simile Remind students that when the words *like* or *as* are used to compare two different things, it is called a *simile*. Guide students in finding a simile in the first verse of the poem. (The poet uses a simile when she says that the lamb's fleece is "white as snow.") They will have more opportunities to work with similes on the second activity page.

Follow-up Activities

Students may work independently to complete the activities on pages 94 and 95.

Mary's Lamb

Mary had a little lamb,
Its fleece was white as snow,
And everywhere that Mary went
The lamb was sure to go;
He followed her to school one day—
That was against the rule,
It made the children laugh and play
To see a lamb at school.

And so the Teacher turned him out,
But still he lingered near,
And waited patiently about,
Till Mary did appear.
And then he ran to her and laid
His head upon her arm,
As if he said—"I'm not afraid—
You'll shield me from all harm."

"What makes the lamb love Mary so?"
The little children cry;
"O, Mary loves the lamb you know,
The Teacher did reply,
"And you each gentle animal
In confidence may bind,
And make them follow at your call,
If you are always kind."

—Sarah Josepha Hale

Understanding the Poem

Read each question and choose the best answer. You may wish to reread "Mary's Lamb" as you work.

1. The lamb followed Mary to _____.

Ⓐ school
Ⓑ the park
Ⓒ the store
Ⓓ her house

2. What did the teacher do when she "turned the lamb out"?

Ⓐ had him join the class
Ⓑ made him turn around
Ⓒ put him on a "timeout"
Ⓓ sent him out of the school

3. In this poem, the word **lingered** means _____.

Ⓐ yelled
Ⓑ jumped
Ⓒ went away
Ⓓ stayed around

4. The teacher tells the children that they should always _____.

Ⓐ go straight home
Ⓑ wash their hands
Ⓒ be kind to animals
Ⓓ do their homework

5. Which word best describes how the lamb felt about Mary?

Ⓐ sad
Ⓑ angry
Ⓒ afraid
Ⓓ trusting

Name _____

Understanding the Poem

1. Mary's lamb had fleece that was "white as snow." This kind of comparison is called a **simile**. On the lines below, create some other similes to describe the lamb.

   The lamb's hooves were as hard as _____.

   The lamb's nose was as soft as _____.

   The lamb's eyes were as bright as _____.

2. A lamb is a baby sheep. Match the name of each animal with the name of its baby.

Animal	Baby
cat	foal
goat	calf
horse	puppy
dog	kitten
goose	kid
cow	gosling

3. If you could have an animal come to visit your classroom, what animal would you choose? Explain your answer.

   _____

   _____

   _____

4. Draw a picture showing the animal in your classroom. Use the other side of this page if you need more room.

Before You Read the Poem

Build Background

The Thanksgiving holiday in the United States traces its origins to 1621, the year the Pilgrims celebrated their first successful harvest. Their governor, William Bradford, asked the Pilgrims to set aside a day to give thanks for their blessings and to share the bountiful crops with the neighboring Native Americans. Tell students that they are going to read the lyrics, or words, to a popular Thanksgiving song that was first published in 1845.

Build Vocabulary

Encourage students to give the meaning for the familiar words on this list; provide simple definitions for any unfamiliar words:

dapple grey: a spotted gray horse

hark: listen

pow: an old-fashioned word meaning "head"

spy: see

'tis: it is

trot: a horse's quick walk

While You Read the Poem

If students know the tune for this song, lead them in a sing-along. If they are reticent about singing, ask them to read the poem together as a class.

After You Read the Poem

Elements of Poetry

Poet's Toolbox: Rhyme Many songs rely on rhyme to help singers remember the words. Remind students that a *rhyme scheme* is the pattern made by the ending rhymes of each line. Work with students to identify the rhyme scheme in the song's first stanza *(abccb)*. After labeling the rhyme scheme for this stanza, have volunteers read the pairs of rhyming words. You may wish to assign one stanza each to individual students or partners and ask them to label the rhyme scheme. Afterwards, they can present their results to the group. They will practice this again on the second activity page.

Follow-up Activities

Students may work independently to complete the activities on pages 99 and 100.

Students may wish to learn more about harvest festivals. Many ancient cultures celebrated the harvest. The Greeks, for example, paid tribute to Demeter, the goddess of grains, each autumn. Similarly, the Romans honored the goddess Ceres in the fall. Many Jewish families still celebrate Sukkoth, a harvest festival that goes back nearly 3,000 years. Invite students to research these and other harvest festivals on the Internet. A good starting site is http://www.holidays.net.

The New-England Boy's Song about
Thanksgiving Day

1 Over the river, and through the wood,
To grandfather's house we go;
The horse knows the way,
To carry the sleigh,
Through the white and drifted snow.

2 Over the river, and through the wood,
To grandfather's house away!
We would not stop
For doll or top,
For 'tis Thanksgiving Day.

3 Over the river, and through the wood,
Oh, how the wind does blow!
It stings the toes,
And bites the nose,
As over the ground we go.

4 Over the river, and through the wood,
With a clear blue winter sky,
The dogs do bark,
And children hark,
As we go jingling by.

5 Over the river, and through the wood,
To have a first-rate play—
Hear the bells ring
Ting a ling ding,
Hurra for Thanksgiving Day!

6 Over the river, and through the wood—
No matter for winds that blow;
Or if we get
The sleigh upset,
Into a bank of snow.

7 Over the river, and through the wood,
         To see little John and Ann;
            We will kiss them all,
            And play snow-ball,
         And stay as long as we can.

8 Over the river, and through the wood,
         Trot fast, my dapple grey!
            Spring over the ground,
            Like a hunting hound,
         For 'tis Thanksgiving Day!

9 Over the river, and through the wood,
      And straight through the barn-yard gate;
            We seem to go
            Extremely slow,
         It is so hard to wait.

10 Over the river, and through the wood,
         Old Jowler hears our bells;
            He shakes his pow,
            with a loud bow-wow,
         and thus the news he tells.

11 Over the river, and through the wood—
      When grandmother sees us come,
            She will say, Oh dear,
            The children are here,
         Bring a pie for every one.

12 Over the river, and through the wood—
         Now grandmother's cap I spy!
            Hurra for the fun!
            Is the pudding done?
         Hurra for the pumpkin pie!

—Lydia Maria Child

Understanding the Poem

Read each question and choose the best answer. You may wish to reread "The New-England Boy's Song about Thanksgiving Day" as you work.

1. In the first stanza, what does the horse know?

   Ⓐ the way to the next-door neighbor's house

   Ⓑ how to pull a sleigh through the snow

   Ⓒ how to get across a river

   Ⓓ the way to carry the cart

2. In stanza 6, what does the word **upset** mean?

   Ⓐ turned over

   Ⓑ crying

   Ⓒ angry

   Ⓓ sad

3. In stanza 7, what game is the narrator going to play with John and Ann?

   Ⓐ soccer

   Ⓑ football

   Ⓒ basketball

   Ⓓ snow-ball

4. What is the "dapple grey" in stanza 8?

   Ⓐ a greyhound dog

   Ⓑ a gray horse

   Ⓒ a gray cat

   Ⓓ a gray car

5. In the last stanza, what traditional Thanksgiving dessert is mentioned?

   Ⓐ sweet potato pie

   Ⓑ mincemeat pie

   Ⓒ pumpkin pie

   Ⓓ apple pie

Understanding the Poem

A **rhyme scheme** is the pattern made by the ending rhymes of each line. For example, the song's first stanza has a rhyme scheme of *abccb*. This means that the second line rhymes with the fifth, and the third line rhymes with the fourth:

Over the river, and through the **wood,**	a
To grandfather's house we **go;**	b
The horse knows the **way,**	c
To carry the **sleigh,**	c
Through the white and drifted **snow.**	b

1. With a partner, write your own stanza to this song. Keep the *abccb* rhyme scheme. Fill in the blanks with your own words.

Over the river, and through the wood,

Oh, how the horse does neigh!

The day is _____.

The meal is _____.

Hurra for Thanksgiving Day!

2. Draw a picture to go with your stanza, or another part of the poem.

Before You Read the Poem

Build Background and Vocabulary

Tell students that the poem they will read next is called "My Country 'Tis of Thee." Read the first three lines aloud, then invite volunteers to share about what these lines might mean. You may need to remind them that *'tis* is an old-fashioned way to say *it is;* students may remember that from "The New-England Boy's Song about Thanksgiving Day." Be sure they know that *thee* is an old-fashioned way to say *you.* Then help students understand that a modern way to say the first three lines is: *My country, it is of you, sweet land of liberty, that I sing.* Encourage students to speculate about the meaning of "sweet land of liberty" and why a poet would sing about that.

While You Read the Poem

Ask students to read the song lyrics through silently several times. You may wish to lead the class in singing the song once or twice. Then invite individuals, partners, or small groups to recite or sing the lyrics.

After You Read the Poem

Elements of Poetry

Poet's Toolbox: Rhyme Scheme Remind students that the rhyme scheme of a poem shows its patterns of rhymes. Together, work through the process of identifying the rhyme scheme in these lyrics by placing a new letter of the alphabet next to each line that ends with a new sound. Place the same letter by lines that end with the same sound as a previous line. So *thee* and *liberty* will both get the letter *a* because the ending sound of *liberty* rhymes with *thee.*

Form: Song This poem was actually written as lyrics for a song. Share the following information with students about Samuel F. Smith, the author of the song: Smith was a minister. In 1832, he was leafing through a book of old German hymns, or church songs, when he found a song with a tune he thought sounded patriotic. Within a half-hour, Smith wrote the entire song on a piece of scrap paper! If you're ever watching the Olympics and an athlete from Great Britain wins the gold medal, you may hear this song when the athlete receives her or his medal. Britain's national anthem and "My Country 'Tis of Thee" have different words, but they are sung to the same tune. The British version is called "God Save the Queen."

Follow-up Activities

Students may work independently to complete the activities on pages 103 and 104.

My Country 'Tis of Thee

My country, 'tis of thee,

Sweet land of liberty,

Of thee I sing;

Land where my fathers died,

Land of the pilgrims' pride,

From every mountainside,

Let freedom ring!

—*Samuel F. Smith*

Read and Understand Poetry • EMC 3323 • ©2005 by Evan-Moor Corp.

Understanding the Poem

Read each question and choose the best answer. You may wish to reread "My Country 'Tis of Thee" as you work.

1. Who is mentioned in the song as feeling proud of America?
- Ⓐ Native Americans
- Ⓑ our fathers
- Ⓒ pilgrims
- Ⓓ soldiers

2. What does the narrator hope for at the end of the song?
- Ⓐ Americans will sing together more.
- Ⓑ Freedom will be found everywhere.
- Ⓒ People will climb more mountains.
- Ⓓ America will become "sweeter."

3. "My Country 'Tis of Thee" is mainly about _____.
- Ⓐ the love of living in a free country
- Ⓑ winning the Revolutionary War
- Ⓒ beautiful areas of the USA
- Ⓓ the joy of singing together

4. Which word means about the same as **liberty**?
- Ⓐ library
- Ⓑ freedom
- Ⓒ loneliness
- Ⓓ happiness

5. Why does the poet say America is the "land where my fathers died"?
- Ⓐ His father and stepfather died in America.
- Ⓑ His father was buried in the soil of America.
- Ⓒ Many Native Americans died as America grew.
- Ⓓ Our forefathers died fighting to make America free.

My Country 'Tis of Thee

Understanding the Poem

1. **Antonyms** are words that have opposite meanings. Match each word from the song to its antonym.

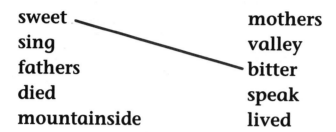

sweet	mothers
sing	valley
fathers	bitter
died	speak
mountainside	lived

2. Poets use rhyming words to create patterns in their writing. Words that rhyme aren't always spelled the same. Read each pair of rhyming words below. Notice the spelling. Then add one more rhyming word to each pair.

thee—sea	**beware—fair**	**sing—wing**
_____	_____	_____
daisy—lazy	**died—sighed**	**done—fun**
_____	_____	_____

3. In this poem, "our fathers" is another way to say "our forefathers." **Forefathers** and **foremothers** are people who lived before you. Write the names of some of your forefathers and foremothers. They can be people in your family or famous people from our country's past.

_____

_____

4. What are some of the things that you love about your country? List them below.

_____

_____

Now, draw one of them on the back of this page.

A World of Sights & Sounds

Contents

Before You Read the Poem

Build Background

Tell students that the following poem is about the Tarahumara Indians of northern Mexico. They call themselves the Raramuri, but foreigners have called them Tarahumara ever since Spanish explorers first gave them this name in the 1500s. Corn is the most important crop of the Tarahumara, and the fall harvest is a major celebration. The Tarahumara are very well known for their ability to run long distances, and they have been invited to join marathons in the United States. This poem celebrates the Tarahumara's way of life.

While You Read the Poem

With students, read the poem aloud several times, exploring its cadence, or inflection in tone, and rhythm. The sound of "pom, pom" may be chanted in the rhythm of a heartbeat. When the class has practiced reciting the poem several times, form two groups of students. Have one group read the text; the other group chants, "pom, pom." Students in the "rhythm group" may also want to pat their legs or devise some other percussive sound to mark the beat as they read.

After You Read the Poem

Elements of Poetry

Poet's Toolbox: Typesetting Sometimes the placement of text on the page is very important for a poem to take its intended effect. Ask students what they notice about the way the text of this poem is laid out. If necessary, point out that the text is centered on the page. In this way, the words "pom, pom" appear at the center of each line. This placement emphasizes that rhythm is a central element of the Tarahumara's way of life. Just by looking at the words of the poem, we can see that the sound of the drum is always at the center of things. The other lines get progressively shorter, and the beat quickens. The reader is also tipped off to this by the visual layout of the text.

Poet's Toolbox: Onomatopoeia Draw students' attention to the "pom, pom" that appears in every other line of the poem. Ask students what they think this sound is supposed to represent. They are likely to say that it represents the sound of a drumbeat. The drumbeat, in turn, represents the sound of a variety of activities: hoeing, patting tortillas, and running. Tell students that the "pom, pom" is an example of *onomatopoeia*. It is a word that sounds like the action it represents. Other examples of onomatopoeia are *knock-knock*, *hiss*, and *crash*. Ask students to brainstorm other words to represent the sound of a drumbeat and practice reciting the poem with their new onomatopoeias.

Follow-up Activities

Students may work independently to complete the activities on pages 108 and 109.

I Hear, I Hear

I hear the rhythm of the Tarahumaras
pom, pom,

I hear them hoeing in the cornfields
pom, pom,

I hear them patting tortillas
pom, pom,

I hear them herding their goats
pom, pom,

I hear their bare feet on the land
pom, pom,

I hear them running, running
pom, pom,

I hear their steady drumbeats
pom, pom,
pom, pom,
pom, pom.

—*Pat Mora*

Understanding the Poem

Read each question and choose the best answer. You may wish to reread "I Hear, I Hear" as you work.

1. Which animals are mentioned in the poem?

(A) cows

(B) goats

(C) sheep

(D) horses

2. Which of these activities comes first in the poem?

(A) hoeing

(B) patting

(C) running

(D) herding

3. This poem is mainly about _____.

(A) how to grow corn

(B) how to make tortillas

(C) the sounds of a forest at night

(D) the everyday life of an Indian tribe

4. The word **bare** in this poem means _____.

(A) without heat

(B) a wild animal

(C) without shoes

(D) a type of berry

5. From the poem, you can tell that the Tarahumara spend a lot of time _____.

(A) in bed

(B) indoors

(C) outdoors

(D) in the city

Read and Understand Poetry • EMC 3323 • ©2005 by Evan-Moor Corp.

Understanding the Poem

1. There are many action words in the poem with an **-ing** ending. These words help to add movement to the poem. Write these action words with an **-ing** ending.

beat	_____	pat	_____
cook	_____	plant	_____
farm	_____	play	_____
herd	_____	run	_____
hoe	_____	sing	_____

2. The poet uses the onomatopoeia **pom, pom** to represent different sounds. How would you represent the sound of the following activities? Be creative and make up your own words!

hoeing cornfields   thunk, thunk _____

patting tortillas   _____

herding goats   _____

running barefoot   _____

3. What are some sounds of life in the city? Read this list of things that make noise, and then write an onomatopoeia showing the sound it makes. Follow the example.

car   honk, honk _____

train   _____

clock   _____

jackhammer   _____

ambulance   _____

Before You Read the Poem

Build Background

On a world map, point out China and Hong Kong. Talk with students about the busy harbors of this region, explaining that there is a lot of boat traffic. There are so many boats going to and fro that smaller boats service them by selling food and merchandise. A sampan, for example, is a small skiff propelled by two oars, and it may or may not have a sail. A sampan may have a shelter on top used by people as their permanent home. If possible, show students a picture of a sampan, such as the one that may be viewed at this Web site: http://www.worldisround.com. Tell students that the poem they are about to read is about a sampan.

While You Read the Poem

Have partners practice reading the poem together. As one student reads, the other can tap out the beat created by the words that are repeated at the end of each line at the beginning and at the end of the poem. They can tap out the beat using a drumstick, or by clapping their hands or snapping their fingers. When they are finished with the first reading, have students switch roles.

After You Read the Poem

Elements of Poetry

Form: List Poem Point out that this poem is written as free verse, so it does not use any special pattern of rhyme or meter. This free verse poem builds its rhythm by listing a series of noun-verb combinations that form a singsong refrain. Help students see how these listing verses make up the first four and the last four lines of this twelve-line poem. The middle four lines contain the only complete sentence in the poem: *Up and down the long green river/Willow branches brush the river.* Here, too, however, a line formed of another noun-verb combination—*Ohe Ohe lanterns quiver*—separates this complete thought, helping to retain the singsong quality created by the listing technique.

Poet's Toolbox: Onomatopoeia Remind students that onomatopoeia is the use of a word that sounds like a noise or sound. *Buzz* and *sizzle* are two examples. Ask students to find other examples of onomatopoeia in the poem, such as *lap, clap, flap,* and *tap.*

Follow-up Activities

Students may work independently to complete the activities on pages 112 and 113.

Sampan

Waves lap lap
Fish fins clap clap
Brown sails flap flap
Chopsticks tap tap
Up and down the long green river
Ohe Ohe lanterns quiver
Willow branches brush the river
Ohe Ohe lanterns quiver
Waves lap lap
Fish fins clap clap
Brown sails flap flap
Chopsticks tap tap

—*Tao Lang Pee*
**translation by
Channing and
Olive Wence**

Sampan

Understanding the Poem

Read each question and choose the best answer. You may wish to reread "Sampan" as you work.

1. The word **quiver** means _____.

- Ⓐ fall
- Ⓑ sleep
- Ⓒ break
- Ⓓ tremble

2. Which words help you know that the poem takes place on or near the water?

- Ⓐ waves, fish, river
- Ⓑ green, brush, tap
- Ⓒ clap, long, branches
- Ⓓ brown, chopsticks, lanterns

3. This poem is about the things you would see and hear _____.

- Ⓐ at school
- Ⓑ on a train
- Ⓒ on a sampan
- Ⓓ on an airplane

4. What color are the sampan's sails?

- Ⓐ pink
- Ⓑ brown
- Ⓒ yellow
- Ⓓ orange

5. What sound is made by the chopsticks?

- Ⓐ lap lap
- Ⓑ tap tap
- Ⓒ flap flap
- Ⓓ clap clap

Read and Understand Poetry • EMC 3323 •

Sampan

Understanding the Poem

1. **Onomatopoeia** is the use of a word that sounds like the thing it tells about. **Crash** is a good example. It is used to tell about an accident at high speed. It sounds like an accident, too!

   What word does the poet use for the sound of:

   a. chopsticks as they click against each other? _____

   b. small waves gently coming up to the riverbank? _____

   c. fish as they flap their fins open and shut? _____

   d. the sails of a boat flapping in the wind? _____

2. Do you know these other examples of onomatopoeia? Choose from the words in the box. Write the best word next to its description.

achoo	buzz	hiss	pitter-pat	splat	whoosh

   a. The sound you make when you sneeze: _____

   b. The sound of an egg falling on the floor: _____

   c. The sound of a snake's tongue flicking in and out: _____

   d. The sound of a cat walking across the roof: _____

   e. The sound of a bee flying around the room: _____

   f. The sound of a hawk swooping through the air: _____

3. What are some of your favorite onomatopoeias? Write a list of at least four good ones. Show them to a classmate and ask him or her to guess what they represent.

   _____

   _____

   _____

   _____

Before You Read the Poem

Build Background

Ask students what they think this poem will be about, based on the title. If necessary, ask questions such as: *Do you think the poem is about the color black? What else do we mean when we use the word* black? Confirm for students that *black* is commonly used in our society when talking about African Americans. Strictly speaking, it refers to skin color, although it is also used when talking about African American heritage and black culture. Ask students if they think the author of this poem is black, and why they think so. It is very probable that students will know in advance that the author is black, and that the poem is about black pride. Ask students to keep this in mind while reading the poem. You might tell them now or after they read the poem that poet Andreya Renee Allen wrote "Black Is Beautiful" when she was a teenager.

While You Read the Poem

Ask several volunteers to demonstrate how they think the poem should be read. The poem invites a rhythmic, almost rap-like reading. Ask one of the volunteers to lead the class in a choral reading of the poem. Conduct this choral reading several times until students are familiar with the poem. Challenge students to read the poem aloud without looking at the text.

After You Read the Poem

Elements of Poetry

Form: Free Verse Tell students that this poem is written as free verse. That means that it does not use any special pattern of rhyme or meter. Invite students to find the places in the poem where there are natural pauses. Although all students may not "hear" pauses in the same places, they should all notice that it sounds awkward and choppy to pause at the end of every line.

Poet's Toolbox: Italics and Boldface Explain to students that italics and boldface are "typesetting tools" poets can use to emphasize words to make them stand out. Point out the use of italics in the third line: "Black is *the* color." Explain that italicized words are read with emphasis. The poet also put certain words in boldface type to make those words stand out. The boldfaced words are also set in a larger size than the rest of the words in the poem. The poet may or may not have intended for the boldfaced words to be read with emphasis or greater volume. It could be that she simply wanted the printed page to have a dynamic, active look that fit the poem. Ask students why they think the poet used boldface in the way she did.

Follow-up Activities

Students may work independently to complete the activities on pages 116 and 117.

Black Is Beautiful

Black is beautiful
Black is me
Black is *the* color
       can't you see
       that

blue **is** nice,
and orange is neat
but they can't compete
       because

Black is beautiful
Black is me

Tall, dark, and wonderful
     see!

—*Andreya Renee Allen*

Understanding the Poem

Read each question and choose the best answer. You may wish to reread "Black Is Beautiful" as you work.

1. In the poem, what color does the speaker mention five times?

Ⓐ blue

Ⓑ black

Ⓒ brown

Ⓓ orange

2. In this poem, the poet is talking about _____ .

Ⓐ skin color

Ⓑ some colors of the rainbow

Ⓒ all the meanings of the word **black**

Ⓓ the differences between colors

3. How does the poet feel about her color?

Ⓐ shy

Ⓑ proud

Ⓒ unconcerned

Ⓓ too good for words

4. Which of these words is a synonym for **beautiful**?

Ⓐ ugly

Ⓑ happy

Ⓒ lovely

Ⓓ helpful

5. Which of these expresses the poet's message?

Ⓐ People are all the same.

Ⓑ Be proud of who you are.

Ⓒ Different colors don't mix.

Ⓓ Don't pay attention to skin color.

Black Is Beautiful

Understanding the Poem

1. List some of the words that the poet uses to describe herself.

_____

2. The author of this poem is black, or African American. What do you know about your racial and cultural background? Write a few lines that tell about your family history and where your ancestors came from.

_____

_____

_____

3. What color is your hair? What color are your eyes? What color is your skin? You may need to look in a mirror. Then draw a picture of yourself. Try to use colors that match yours. You may need to mix colors.

_____

4. Write something about yourself or your background that makes you feel proud.

_____

_____

Before You Read the Poems

Build Background

Read aloud "Worm," the first poem in the haiku collection. Ask students to close their eyes and form a picture of the image that the poem creates as you read it aloud. Then have students open their eyes and share the feelings and images they experienced. The late-night setting and attention to minute detail might create a feeling of peace and quiet. Tell students that this haiku is by the poet Basho. He lived in Japan from 1644 to 1695, and he was a master of haiku. Traditionally, this poetic form was used to capture the essence of a moment in nature. Some haiku can also be humorous, and this is especially true of modern haiku. The other two poems in the collection are by modern poets. One follows the traditional theme of nature. The other shows how haiku can capture a "humorous moment" in everyday activities.

While You Read the Poems

Have volunteers take turns reading each haiku aloud. Remind students that they need not pause at the end of each line. Sentences may flow from one line to the next. Haiku is too short to set a rhythm, and it often sounds like a simple statement when read aloud. Invite students to read each poem aloud several times, changing their delivery to achieve the reading that is most suited to it.

After You Read the Poems

Elements of Poetry

Form: Haiku Write one of the poems on the board and have students help you count the number of syllables in each line. Make a slash after each syllable, showing students that the first and last lines have five syllables, and the second line has seven syllables. Have partners count syllables in "Dawn Haiku" to see if it matches this pattern. They will practice counting the syllables in "Cookery Haiku" on the second activity page.

Form: Translation Tell students that haiku poetry can be very difficult to translate into English. The Japanese language doesn't have an alphabet like English, and these short poems are packed with meaning. It is a challenge to make the poems fit the five-seven-five syllable pattern in translation while keeping the same meaning. Ask students if the translation of Basho's haiku succeeded in matching the traditional pattern.

Poet's Toolbox: Imagery Tell students that poets often use descriptive words to create pictures in the reader's mind. Ask them to describe the pictures they see in their mind when you read these phrases: "dawn is delicious soup," "planet pizza," and "seas of cheese are melting."

Follow-up Activities

Students may work independently to complete the activities on pages 120 and 121.

Worm

At night, quietly,
a worm under the moonlight
digs into a nut.

—*Basho*

Cookery Haiku

On planet pizza
Seas of cheese are melting tide
On tomato shores

—*John Calvert*

Dawn Haiku

dawn is delicious
soup made from dew and birdsong
drink it with your ears

—*Sue Cowling*

Understanding the Poems

Read each question and choose the best answer. You may wish to reread the three haiku as you work.

1. What is Basho's message in his haiku?
- Ⓐ Creatures do weird things at night.
- Ⓑ It is easy to see in the moonlight.
- Ⓒ There is beauty in small things.
- Ⓓ Worms like eating nuts.

2. What does Sue Cowling say **dawn** is made from?
- Ⓐ delicious soup
- Ⓑ sunshine and birdsong
- Ⓒ wonderful things for your ears
- Ⓓ morning dew and songs of birds

3. Which of these is <u>not</u> mentioned by John Calvert in his haiku?
- Ⓐ the melting cheese
- Ⓑ the hot, crunchy crust
- Ⓒ the shape of the pizza
- Ⓓ the tomato sauce topping

4. You can tell from Sue Cowling's haiku that she _____.
- Ⓐ likes to eat soup
- Ⓑ can't use her mouth to drink
- Ⓒ has tried to make soup using dew
- Ⓓ enjoys the sights and sounds of sunrise

5. You can tell from Basho's haiku that he probably _____.
- Ⓐ has sat out under a moonlit sky
- Ⓑ never stays up late at night
- Ⓒ has a fear of worms
- Ⓓ likes to eat nuts

Read and Understand Poetry • EMC 3323 • ©2005 by Evan-Moor Corp.

Understanding the Poems

1. The message of a haiku can be changed into a few sentences. Read the following example:

The message of "Dawn Haiku" is:

___Early morning is a wonderful time. The grass is wet and___
___birds are singing. Enjoy what you hear.___

Now, you try writing the message of these haiku in one or two sentences.

The message of "Worm" is:

_____

_____

The message of "Cookery Haiku" is:

_____

_____

2. Practice counting the syllables in "Cookery Haiku." Make a mark above each syllable in each word. Count the syllables in each line. Write the number of syllables after each line.

    On planet pizza   _____

    Seas of cheese are melting tide   _____

    On tomato shores   _____

3. What did you "see" when you read the three haiku? Draw a picture on the back of this page to go with one of the haiku. Be creative!

Alliteration (uh-lih-tuh-RAY-shun)

When several words that begin with the same sound are next to each other or close together, it is called **alliteration**. In this example, the words **sly, sleek,** and **slips** create alliteration.

Example:

Sly and sleek,
it slips away.

*from "The Snake"
by Janet Lawler*

Boldface and Italics

When words are printed in **boldface,** they are in darker, heavier type. Boldface is used to help words stand out better and add emphasis. Words are sometimes set in *italic* type as another way to add emphasis. The word **the** is printed in italics in the example shown.

Example:

Black is beautiful
Black is me
Black is *the* color

*from "Black Is Beautiful"
by Andreya Renee Allen*

Capitalization and Punctuation

When writing poetry, some authors choose not to use **capitalization** or **punctuation.** The rules for using capital letters and punctuation marks are not as strict in poetry.

Example:

i will kiss your cool bark
and hug you safe and tight

*from "little tree"
by E. E. Cummings*

Concrete Poem

A poem that is written with words that form a shape is called a **concrete poem.** Usually, the shape of the poem is similar to the subject of the poem, as in this poem about going up a staircase.

Example:

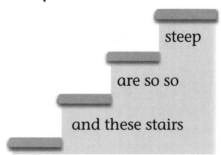

steep
are so so
and these stairs

*from "Up the Stairs to Bed"
by Ian Souter*

Couplet (CUP-lit)

When two lines in a poem rhyme, they are called a **couplet**. (Do you see the word **couple** in this word? **Couple** also means "two.") This example includes two couplets.

Example:

In winter I get up at night
And dress by yellow candle-light.
In summer quite the other way,
I have to go to bed by day.

from "Bed in Summer"
by Robert Louis Stevenson

Free Verse

When a poem is written without a pattern of rhyme, meter, or line length, it is called **free verse**. Poets use words and images to help make free verse feel different from regular sentences, or **prose**.

Example:

I would love to be a horse;
to race along the shore,
the wind in my mane.

from "I Would Love to Be a Horse"
by Linda Armstrong

Haiku (hi-KOO)

Haiku is a form of poetry that first began in Japan in the 1700s. A haiku always has three lines. In the "classic" form, the first and third lines have five syllables, and the second line has seven. A traditional haiku focuses on an image in nature. Even when haiku does not focus on nature, it usually presents a closeup look at a single detail.

Example:

At night, quietly,
a worm under the moonlight
digs into a nut.

"Worm"
by Basho

Hyperbole (hi-PUR-buh-lee)

When a writer exaggerates on purpose, it is called **hyperbole**. Hyperbole is often used to add humor to poetry. In this example, it is a wild exaggeration that "all the birds of the air" might ever be able to sit on a bonnet.

Example:

All the birds of the air
Are welcome to sit on my bonnet!

from "Limerick 1,"
The Book of Nonsense,
by Edward Lear

Imagery (IH-muh-jree)

Imagery is what we call the words or phrases used by writers to help readers make pictures in their mind. What do you see when you read the imagery used by John Calvert in "Cookery Haiku"?

Example:

On planet pizza
Seas of cheese are melting tide
On tomato shores

"Cookery Haiku"
by John Calvert

Innovation (ih-no-VAY-shun)

When a writer makes changes to a work that already exists in order to create a different work, we call it an **innovation.** Compare the stanza from John Himmelman's innovation to the stanza from the original nursery rhyme to see how the poet changed the existing work.

Example:

Ladybug, Ladybug
Fly away home.
Your house is on fire,
And your children all gone.

from a traditional nursery rhyme

Ladybug, Ladybug
Stay right here.
Don't fly home,
You have nothing to fear.

from "Ladybug, Ladybug"
by John Himmelman

Internal Rhyme

When words that are part of the same line of a poem rhyme with each other, it is called **internal rhyme. Internal** means "inside." In this example, the first line has internal rhyme. The first and second lines also rhyme with each other.

Example:

Crunch, munch,
Have some lunch!

from "July"
by Lana Krumwiede

Limerick (LIH-muh-rick)

Limericks are silly or nonsensical rhymes that follow a very specific rhyme scheme. Limericks always have five lines. The first, second, and fifth lines always rhyme. The third and fourth lines also rhyme. Limericks always follow the same pattern of meter as you find in this limerick by Edward Lear.

Example:

There was a young lady whose eyes
Were unique as to color and size.
When she opened them wide
People all turned aside
And started away in surprise.

from "Limerick 3," The Book of Nonsense, by Edward Lear

Lyric Poetry (LIH-rick)

Poetry that focuses on feelings is called **lyric poetry**. When they read a lyric poem, readers may think about similar feelings and experiences they have had, or they may imagine the feelings described by the poet. When you read this short lyric poem, do you feel how the poet longs for summer to come again? Have you ever had that feeling when you know that summer is ending?

Example: Fly away, fly away over the sea,
Sun-loving swallow, for summer is done;
Come again, come again, come back to me,
Bringing the summer, and bringing the sun.

*"The Swallow"
by Christina Rossetti*

Lyrics

When the words of a poem are set to music and sung, they are called **lyrics**. Sometimes, the words and the music are created separately and combined later. Sometimes, the words and music are created at the same time. When the following lyrics were written in 1845, they were meant to be sung.

Example: Over the river, and through the wood,
To grandfather's house we go;

*from "The New-England Boy's Song about Thanksgiving Day"
by Lydia Maria Child*

Meter (MEE-tur)

A regular pattern of rhythm is called **meter**. Writing made up of sentences that use meter is called **verse**. Writing made up of sentences that do <u>not</u> use meter is called **prose**.

Example:

See **Limerick** (previous page) for an example of a poem that has a special **meter**, or pattern of rhythm.

Onomatopoeia (aw-nuh-mah-tuh-PEE-uh)

When a word sounds like the noise or sound that it stands for, it is called **onomatopoeia**. **Buzz** and **sizzle** are examples of onomatopoeia. In the following lines, the words **lap**, **clap**, **flap**, and **tap** are examples of onomatopoeia.

Example:

Waves lap lap
Fish fins clap clap
Brown sails flap flap
Chopsticks tap tap

from "Sampan"
by Tao Lang Pee

Personification (per-sawn-uh-fuh-KAY-shun)

When a writer describes something that is not human as having qualities or capabilities that are human, it is called **personification.** In this example from the poem "Ladybug, Ladybug," the poet uses personification in describing the ladybug's family.

Example:

Your children are sleeping.
Your husband is shopping.
Your father is sweeping.
Your mother is mopping.

from "Ladybug, Ladybug"
by John Himmelman

Repetition (reh-peh-TIH-shun)

When a poet uses the same word or words more than once in a line or in a poem, it is called **repetition.** Repetition can be used to emphasize a word or an idea in a poem. Repetition can also be used to create special sounds or rhythms in a poem. In this example, the subject of the poem is repeated once or twice in each line.

Example:

Pumpkins oval, pumpkins round,
Pumpkins tumbling on the ground;

from "Pumpkins"
by Virginia Kroll

Rhyme

When two words end with the same sound, we say they **rhyme**. Poets use rhyming words to help make their writing sound different from prose. Rhyme can help words sound special or more musical. Rhyming words are usually placed at the end of a line in a poem.

Example: For his Hat was a hundred and two feet wide,
            With ribbons and bibbons on every side

from "The Quangle Wangle's Hat"
by Edward Lear

Rhyme Scheme

When a poet uses a special pattern of rhyming words in a poem, it is called a **rhyme scheme**. You can use letters to help you figure out the rhyme scheme in a poem. Give lines that end with the same rhyme pattern the same letter. In this example, **swing** and **thing** follow the same rhyme pattern, and **blue** and **do** follow another rhyme pattern. So we say that this stanza has an *abab* rhyme scheme.

Example: How do you like to go up in a swing,
            Up in the air so blue?
            Oh, I do think it the pleasantest thing
            Ever a child can do!

from "The Swing"
by Robert Louis Stevenson

Rhythm (RIH-thum)

The sound of accented and unaccented syllables in words creates **rhythm.** The rhythm of a poem can be felt in its words and in the pauses that come between them. Rhythm helps give poetry a musical quality. As you read this example, clap or tap a steady beat. Notice how some of the words fall right on the beat and some do not. Which words are more important in this poem?

Example: There was a little girl,
            Who had a little curl,
            Right in the middle of her forehead.

from "There Was a Little Girl"
by Henry Wadsworth Longfellow

Simile (SIH-muh-lee)

A **simile** compares one thing to another using the word **like** or **as**. In this example, lines of cars on a hilly road are compared to a mechanical caterpillar.

Example: Lines of cars inch along in the fog
Rising and dipping with the humps of the road
Like a mechanical caterpillar.

from "Fog"
by Nancy R. Wadhams

Stanza (STAN-zuh)

A **stanza** is a group of lines in a poem. Usually, the lines in a stanza are related to each other in the same way that the sentences of a paragraph "go together."

Example:

Your children are sleeping.
Your husband is shopping.
Your father is sweeping.
Your mother is mopping. } 1

Your grandma is strumming.
Your grandpa is clapping.
Your auntie is humming.
Your uncle is napping. } 2

from "Ladybug, Ladybug"
by John Himmelman

Translation (trans-LAY-shun)

In a **translation**, words that were originally written in one language are expressed in another language. In this example, you can compare the original words in Spanish with the translation into English.

Example: De colores,
de colores se visten los campos en la primavera.

Bright with colors,
bright with colors are fields that dress themselves up in the spring.

from "De colores," a traditional Mexican song

Andreya Renee Allen

Andreya Renee Allen was born in 1984. Originally from South Carolina, she has traveled extensively and enjoys meeting new and exciting people, especially readers of all types of literature. She wrote the poem in this book when she was a teenager. She has also written for online magazines. Andreya's goals include being a singer, a part-time writer, and the first black president of the United States.

Linda Armstrong

Linda Armstrong started composing verses before she could write. She remembers sitting in the back seat of the family car inventing rhyming chants during family outings. She wrote poems on scraps of paper all through school, and she continued to write after graduating from college with a degree in English. Her first published poems appeared in <u>The National Anthology of High School Poetry</u>, and a collection of her poetry, <u>Early Tigers</u>, was published in 1995.

Basho

Basho is the pen name of Matsuo Munefusa, a Japanese poet who is considered the finest writer of haiku. He lived during the mid-17th century, when the haiku form was first developed. Basho expressed universal themes using the simple images of nature. His skillful focus on the natural world helped transform haiku from an unimportant pastime into a major form of Japanese poetry.

John Calvert

John Calvert is a British poet. He has contributed poetry and music for all ages to a wide variety of publications and performances.

Lydia Maria Child

Lydia Maria Child was a successful American writer who lived from 1802 to 1880. She wrote the first historical novel published in the United States based on her firsthand knowledge of Native American life. She was the editor of a childen's magazine, and published material for many audiences during her long, productive life. She was active in working to end slavery and in seeking fair treatment of Native Americans and women. Despite her many impressive accomplishments, she is most famous today as the author of the poem found in this book, "The New-England Boy's Song about Thanksgiving Day."

Sue Cowling

Sue Cowling is a British poet. A former teacher, she wrote her first poem when she was nine. She prefers children's poems to poetry for adults.

E. E. Cummings

E. E. Cummings was an important American poet of the 20th century. He also was known for his paintings. In his poetry, Cummings experimented with words and sentences, creating new ways to spell and write. Even though the forms Cummings used were new and different, his poetry is written in language that is easy to understand. The subjects of his poems are also easy to understand. Cummings was very popular during his lifetime.

Robert Frost

Robert Frost was one of the major American poets of the 20th century. His poems are most often associated with New England life. His poetry nearly always was written in traditional verse forms. The language of his poems shows his wonderful sense of rhythm and meter. Frost was also a master at capturing everyday language and ways of speaking in his poetry.

Sarah Josepha Hale

Sarah Josepha Hale was a magazine editor for most of her life. This was a very important position for a woman in America in the mid-1800s, when most women were not allowed to hold important positions in the workplace. Unlike Mary (of "Mary's Lamb"), Sarah Josepha Hale did not go to school. She was taught at home by her mother and later by her brother. She continued her education on her own and was an outspoken supporter for the rights of women.

John Himmelman

John Himmelman is an award-winning artist and author whose work is influenced by his love of nature. He has written and/or illustrated over 50 books for children. He has said, "I've been playing with insects since I was a kid. My interest in moths probably evolved along with my tendency to stay up late at night. The fact that I could find hundreds of different kinds in my own backyard, and that I find their form, function, and beauty a marvel, helped make them an obsession." Himmelman lives in Killingworth, Connecticut.

Mary Howitt

Mary Howitt was a British poet who lived from 1799 to 1888. Her love of nature and the countryside influenced much of her poetry.

Virginia Kroll

Virginia Kroll is a former teacher. She is the author of more than 20 picture books and has won an American Book Award for excellence in multicultural literature. She now writes full time from her home in New York.

Lana Krumwiede

Lana Krumwiede writes poems and stories for children. Her work has appeared in magazines and other collections. She also teaches writing.

Janet Lawler

Janet Lawler began writing poetry for family greeting cards when she was in elementary school. Despite this early beginning as a poet, she worked as a lawyer for 15 years before becoming a full-time children's author. Ms. Lawler lives in Connecticut with her husband, two children, a dog, two lizards, and two toads. Her love of nature inspires much of her writing.

Edward Lear

Edward Lear (1812–1888) lived in England during the reign of Queen Victoria. He was best known during his lifetime as an illustrator, focusing especially on scientific depiction of birds and other wildlife. Since his death, however, he has become known mainly for mastering the whimsical form known as the **limerick**, as well as for his other humorous poems. While the subject and form of his works vary, nearly all are characterized by an irreverent view of the world. Lear poked fun at everything, including himself.

Henry Wadsworth Longfellow

Henry Wadsworth Longfellow lived from 1807 to 1882. He was one of America's best-loved poets. His poetry is easily understood, with simple, familiar themes. Most people enjoy the patterns of rhythm and rhyme in his poems. He was one of the first artists to use American history, culture, landscape, and traditions as a focus in his art.

Beverly McLoughland

Beverly McLoughland loves to read and write poetry. A collection of her poems has been published, and many of her poems have appeared in magazines and anthologies for children. She often stays up long past midnight writing poetry. It would not be unusual, she says, to find her at the kitchen table, pencil in one hand writing verses, and the other hand reaching for a chocolate donut or a cold glass of milk.

Pat Mora

Pat Mora is an award-winning author of poetry, nonfiction, and children's books. She has published over 20 books for young readers, and often speaks at schools and conferences about writing and multicultural education. A native of El Paso, Texas, she now divides her time between Santa Fe, New Mexico, and Cincinnati, Ohio.

Tao Lang Pee

Little is known about the life of Chinese poet Tao Lang Pee, who was born in 403 B.C. The poem in this book, "Sampan," appears to have been introduced to the Western world by the noted British playwright, Noel Coward. Coward included translations of three poems by Tao Lang Pee in an anthology of poems first published in 1932. The rich and varied Asian images of Tao Lang Pee's poetry can be found today in several poetry collections.

Christina Rossetti

Christina Rossetti was one of the more important English women poets of the Victorian era. She came from an artistic and religious family; all of her brothers were writers or painters. A somber, religious tone can be found in much of her poetry. She often wrote about unhappy love and death.

Martin Shaw

Martin Shaw taught school for 39 years. He is now retired from teaching and is the grandfather of twin girls. He continues to write poetry for children. Many of his poems can be found in anthologies of children's poetry.

Samuel F. Smith

Samuel F. Smith graduated from Harvard University in 1829, then studied to become a minister at Andover Theological Seminary. While at Andover, he wrote verses for a songbook to be used in schools. In 1831, Smith was so inspired by the tune of a patriotic German song that he took up pen and paper and wrote his own patriotic hymn to the same melody. Within a half hour, Smith had written his best-known song: "My Country 'Tis of Thee."

Ian Souter

Ian Souter is a teacher and a writer from Great Britain. His hobbies include sports, computers, photography, music, and reading. His favorite poets are Stanley Cook and Shel Silverstein.

Robert Louis Stevenson

Robert Louis Stevenson is best known today as the author of adventure novels, especially <u>Treasure Island</u>, <u>Kidnapped</u>, and <u>The Strange Case of Dr. Jekyll and Mr. Hyde</u>. During his childhood, Stevenson was ill with tuberculosis, and he spent many long days in bed composing stories and reading. In an attempt to improve his health, he traveled to warmer countries. Those experiences provided rich material for his writing.

Nancy R. Wadhams

As an elementary school teacher, Nancy Wadhams loved introducing poetry to her young students. She still has her worn copy of <u>Silver Pennies</u>, the poetry book that she used as a fourth-grader more than 50 years ago. The sounds and rhythms of poetry sneak into all her writing, even into picture books and novels. Ms. Wadhams lives in Connecticut, but she often travels to Georgia, where she enjoys reciting poetry with her young grandson.

My Read & Understand

Poetry Anthology

This book belongs to:

_____

PARTS OF A POEM

Title
Most poems have a **title**. Some do not. →

Bed in Summer

Line
Poems are usually made up of **lines**. Lines may be organized in stanzas. →

In winter I get up at night   *a*
And dress by yellow candle-light.   *a*
In summer quite the other way,   *b*
I have to go to bed by day.   *b*

Rhyme Scheme
The pattern of rhyming lines in a poem is called the **rhyme scheme**. To show the rhyme scheme, use a different letter to label each line that ends with a new sound.

Stanza
A **stanza** is a group of lines in a poem. The lines go together like sentences in a paragraph. This poem has three stanzas. →

I have to go to bed and see   *c*
The birds still hopping on the tree,   *c*
Or hear the grown-up people's feet   *d*
Still going past me in the street.   *d*

Couplet
When two lines in a poem rhyme, it is called a **couplet**. There are two couplets in this stanza. →

And does it not seem hard to you,   *e*
When all the sky is clear and blue,   *e*
And I should like so much to play,   *b*
To have to go to bed by day?   *b*

—*Robert Louis Stevenson*

Poet
The name of the **poet**, or author of the poem, may go here or before the beginning of the poem. Sometimes, the author of a poem is unknown.

TYPES OF POEMS

Free Verse

A poem written in **free verse** does not follow a pattern of rhyme or rhythm.

little tree

little tree
little silent Christmas tree
you are so little
you are more like a flower

from "little tree" by E. E. Cummings

Limerick

A **limerick** is a funny or silly poem. Limericks always have five lines. The lines always have this rhyme scheme: *aabba*. The rhythm in a limerick is made by a pattern of accents on the syllables in each line. The syllables in boldface will help you see the pattern in this limerick.

Limerick 1

There **was** a young **la**dy whose **bon**net
Came un**tied** when the **birds** sat u**pon** it.
But she **said**, "I don't **care**!
All the **birds** of the **air**
Are **wel**come to **sit** on my **bon**net!"

—Edward Lear

Haiku

Haiku poems always have three lines. The first and last lines have 5 syllables. The second line has 7 syllables. The lines do not rhyme. Haiku poetry is often about something in nature. The syllables are marked in this haiku so you can count them.

Worm

At / night, / qui / et / ly,	5 syllables
a / worm / un / der / the / moon / light	7 syllables
digs / in / to / a / nut.	5 syllables

—Basho

Online Resources

The Academy of American Poets: http://www.poets.org

This comprehensive Web site includes over 1,400 poems, 500 poet biographies, and 100 audio clips of 20th- and 21st-century poets reading their own works (e.g., Gwendolyn Brooks, E. E. Cummings, Robert Frost, Langston Hughes, William Carlos Williams, and others). This site also includes the following:

- the Online Poetry Classroom, with free access to poetry curriculum units and other educational resources for teachers

- the National Poetry Almanac and Calendar, which track poetry-related events nationwide throughout the year

- information on National Poetry Month (April)

Lee & Low Books: http://www.leeandlow.com

Publishers of multicultural literature for children, Lee & Low Books has excellent poetry-related material on the Poetry Power page of their Web site. You'll find the following:

- ideas for bringing poetry into the classroom, by poet Pat Mora and literacy educator Regie Routman

- information on additional resources for incorporating poetry into primary classrooms

- digital movies of contemporary poets of color reading their works, including Tony Medina reading "My Grandmother Had One Good Coat" (included in *Read and Understand Poetry, Grades 5–6*) and Pat Mora reading "Song to Mothers" (included in *Read and Understand Poetry, Grades 2–3*).

Audio Resources

In Their Own Voices—A Century of Recorded Poetry, ©1996, WEA/Atlantic/Rhino

This four-CD boxed set includes 122 poems recorded by their authors, including Robert Frost, Walt Whitman, William Carlos Williams (reading "The Red Wheelbarrow," included in *Read and Understand Poetry, Grades 5–6*), and contemporary poets such as Maya Angelou, Lucille Clifton, Gary Snyder, Carmen Tafolla, and others. In compiling this impressive collection, poetry historian and recording producer Rebekah Presson drew from the Library of Congress archives, poets' personal archives, and recordings made on her 1980s radio show, *New Letters on the Air*. The collection also includes a printed booklet with additional information. Check your public library for a copy of this excellent collection.

The Writer's Almanac®

This is a short program (about five minutes in length) of poetry and history hosted by Garrison Keillor, heard daily on public radio stations. Check their Web site at http:writersalmanac. publicradio.org for local station listings. The Web site also has searchable archives.

Print Resources

Writing Poetry with Children by Jo Ellen Moore, ©1999 by Evan-Moor Corporation

Step-by-step lessons provide guidance for introducing a variety of poetic forms and supporting primary-age students in producing original poetry in each form.

Teaching 10 Fabulous Forms of Poetry by Paul Janeczko, ©2000 by Scholastic

Geared for intermediate grades (4–8), this volume introduces 10 poetic forms and supports students in planning and writing original poetry in each form.

See also the many fine poetry resource books listed on the Web sites noted above.

Ladybug, Ladybug

Page 8

1. D—sweeping
2. C—nephew
3. A—strumming
4. D—stay where she is
5. B—calm

Page 9

1. Answers may include any 3 pairs: here/fear, sleeping/sweeping, shopping/mopping, strumming/humming, clapping/napping, riding/hiding, cooking/looking; accept any additional rhyming words, such as *clear, keeping, hopping, coming, wrapping, sliding, hooking.*
2. children, husband, father, mother, grandma, grandpa, auntie, uncle, brother, sister, niece, nephew
3. Answers should include –*ing* verbs such as *crawling, flying, eating, resting,* etc.
4. Drawings will vary.

The Snake

Page 12

1. B—snake
2. C—find a place to hide
3. D—afraid
4. A—rough
5. C—happy

Page 13

1. Circled: snake, cycle, sack, city, center, slither, circle, sly, safe
2. **toe:** go, slow, know, so; **glide:** hide; **away:** today; other answers will vary, but should rhyme with prompts.
3. slick, silent; slow, sliding; slithers, so; sly, sleek
4. Answers will vary.

Fly Away, Fly Away

Page 16

1. C—summer
2. D—sun-loving
3. A—because summer is over
4. B—ocean
5. A—wants the swallow to come back

Page 17

1. Answers will vary.
2. Answers will vary.
3. Answers and drawings will vary.

I Would Love to Be a Horse

Page 20

1. C—a horse
2. A—ocean waves
3. D—running on the beach
4. B—feet
5. C—running

Page 21

1. Answers will vary.
2. Answers will vary.
3. Answers will vary.
4. Answers and drawings will vary.

The Spider and the Fly

Page 25

1. B—The spider is smarter than the fly.
2. D—She started to believe the spider's compliments.
3. C—Don't be fooled by flattering remarks.
4. A—spins a new web
5. D—mirror

Page 26

1. a. clever
   b. lovely
   c. compliments
2. Answers will vary.
3. Responses will vary.

April's Trick
Page 30
1. C—It's ripped.
2. D—yellow and green
3. A—April 1
4. D—because the bad things aren't true
5. C—an April Fools' joke that someone played

Page 31
1. Answers will vary.
2. Answers and drawings will vary.

Bed in Summer
Page 34
1. C—birds
2. A—a child's feelings about bedtime
3. D—go to bed while it's still light outside
4. C—jumping
5. B—people passing by

Page 35
1. Answers will vary, but should include any 3 of the following: night–candle-light; way–day; see–tree; feet–street; you–blue; play–day.
2. Answers will vary.
3. Answers will vary.
4. Drawings will vary.

July
Page 38
1. C—in the park
2. B—eat
3. A—on the Fourth of July
4. D—enjoys the Fourth of July holiday
5. C—noisy and colorful

Page 39
1. Answers will vary.
2. Answers will vary, but should include any 3 of the following: crunch, whizzle, fizzle, sizzle, tooting, hooting, booming, zooming.
3. Answers will vary.
4. Drawings will vary.

Pumpkins
Page 42
1. B—purple
2. D—right, wrong
3. C—autumn
4. A—select a pumpkin
5. B—scary

Page 43
1. Drawings and labels will vary.
2. At Halloween the spooks are out,
   Bats and broomsticks fly <u>about</u>.
   Costumed kids go door to door
   Collecting candy, treats, and <u>more</u>.
   A haunted house, a creepy sight,
   Scares the children through the <u>night</u>.
   The ghouls that make you scream and run
   Also make Halloween <u>fun</u>!

little tree
Page 46
1. C—the narrator
2. D—tree decorations
3. B—tree branches
4. B—the tree
5. A—when the tree is decorated

Page 47
1. Drawings will vary.
2. Answers will vary.
3. Circled: tinsel, glass ornaments, lights, a bright star
   Crossed out: pinecones, pine needles, branches, coal

The Quangle Wangle's Hat
Page 52
1. A—jam and jelly and bread
2. D—Mr. and Mrs. Canary
3. B—hat
4. C—happy
5. D—balloons

Page 53
1. Drawings will vary.
2. Responses will vary.

Read and Understand Poetry • EMC 3323 • ©2005 by Evan-Moor Corp.

Limerick Collection
Page 56
1. C—green
2. B—The birds sat on it.
3. A—eat
4. D—very strange
5. B—She likes birds very much.

Page 57
1. Drawings will vary.
2. Responses may vary, but could include *bed,* *lump,* and *head.*
3. Limericks will vary, but should follow the correct rhyme scheme *(aabba)* and meter.

Up the Stairs to Bed
Page 60
1. C—sleepy
2. D—high
3. C—a tired child climbing stairs on the way to bed
4. B—energetic
5. A—awake

Page 61
1. Answers will vary.
2. Poems will vary.

There Was a Little Girl
Page 64
1. D—in the center of her forehead
2. C—is well-behaved sometimes
3. B—scream and cry
4. D—He knows she can't always be good.
5. C—wonderful

Page 65
1. girl, pearl, curl, and whirl;
   bite, right, white, light;
   should, wood, good, could
2. Answers will vary.
3. Drawings will vary.

The Swing
Page 69
1. A—a river, trees, and cattle
2. C—playing on a swing
3. D—enjoyable
4. B—blue
5. D—in the country

Page 70
1. Answers will vary, but should convey the idea that it is pleasant and fun.
2. Answers should include *blue, green,* and *brown;* other answers will vary.
3. all, down, countryside, do; remaining answers will vary, but should rhyme.
4. Answers will vary.

Fog
Page 73
1. A—the fog makes it hard for drivers to see
2. B—move along slowly
3. D—how cars in the fog look like a slow-moving caterpillar
4. C—dipping
5. A—an inchworm

Page 74
1. The runner was as fast as a <u>cheetah</u>.
   My best friend is as funny as a <u>clown</u>.
   My coach is as strong as a <u>lion</u>.
   The sun is like a yellow <u>balloon</u>.
   The lights on the cars were like <u>stars</u>.
2. Answers will vary.
3. Drawings will vary.

Concrete Poem
Page 77
1. D—a slide
2. C—slick slide
3. A—playing on a slide
4. D—alliteration
5. C—slippery

Page 78
Poems will vary.

The Pasture

Page 81

1. D—the narrator
2. C—rake out leaves
3. C—on a farm in the country
4. B—sways
5. B—The calf needs washing.

Page 82

1. spring: stream
   pasture: field
   fetch: get
2. Circled: away–may; young–tongue
   Crossed out: wait–watch; gone–long;
   rake–away; come–too
3. Drawings will vary.

Hush, Little Baby

Page 86

1. B—ring
2. D—a mirror
3. C—a horse and cart
4. A—a small wagon
5. B—going to

Page 87

Responses will vary.

Bright with Colors

Page 90

1. C—sunsets
2. D—green
3. D—bright with colors
4. B—spring
5. A—a red bird

Page 91

1. Answers will vary.
2. Answers will vary, but should reflect the idea
   that foliage and blossoms begin to appear
   in spring.
3. Circled: a sunflower, a hummingbird, fire,
   a sunrise, grass
4. Drawings will vary.

Mary's Lamb

Page 94

1. A—school
2. D—sent him out of the school
3. D—stayed around
4. C—be kind to animals
5. D—trusting

Page 95

1. Answers will vary.
2.

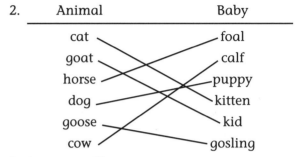

Animal	Baby
cat	foal
goat	calf
horse	puppy
dog	kitten
goose	kid
cow	gosling

3. Answers will vary.
4. Drawings will vary.

The New-England Boy's Song about Thanksgiving Day

Page 99

1. B—how to pull a sleigh through the snow
2. A—turned over
3. D—snow-ball
4. B—a gray horse
5. C—pumpkin pie

Page 100

1. Answers will vary.
2. Drawings will vary.

My Country 'Tis of Thee

Page 103

1. C—pilgrims
2. B—Freedom will be found everywhere.
3. A—the love of living in a free country
4. B—freedom
5. D—Our forefathers died fighting to make
   America free.

Read and Understand Poetry • EMC 3323 • ©2005 by Evan-Moor Corp.

Page 104

1. sweet — lived
   sing — bitter
   fathers — speak
   died — mothers
   mountainside — valley

   (matching lines crossing to: sweet–lived, sing–bitter, fathers–speak, died–mothers, mountainside–valley)

2. Answers will vary, but should rhyme.
3. Answers will vary.
4. Answers and drawings will vary.

I Hear, I Hear
Page 108

1. B—goats
2. A—hoeing
3. D—the everyday life of an Indian tribe
4. C—without shoes
5. C—outdoors

Page 109

1. beating, patting, cooking, planting, farming, playing, herding, running, hoeing, singing
2. Answers will vary.
3. Answers will vary.

Sampan
Page 112

1. D—tremble
2. A—waves, fish, river
3. C—on a sampan
4. B—brown
5. B—tap tap

Page 113

1. a. tap tap
   b. lap lap
   c. clap clap
   d. flap flap
2. a. achoo
   b. splat
   c. hiss
   d. pitter-pat
   e. buzz
   f. whoosh
3. Answers will vary.

Black Is Beautiful
Page 116

1. B—black
2. A—skin color
3. B—proud
4. C—lovely
5. A—Be proud of who you are.

Page 117

1. Answers will vary, but should include any of the following: beautiful, tall, dark, wonderful.
2. Answers will vary.
3. Drawings will vary.
4. Answers will vary.

Haiku Collection
Page 120

1. C—There is beauty in small things.
2. D—morning dew and songs of birds
3. B—the hot, crunchy crust
4. D—enjoys the sights and sounds of sunrise
5. A—has sat out under a moonlit sky

Page 121

1. Answers will vary.
2. On planet pizza _____5_____
   Seas of cheese are melting tide _____7_____
   On tomato shores _____5_____
3. Drawings will vary.

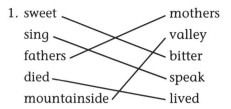

Read and Understand Poetry • EMC 3323 • ©2005 by Evan-Moor Corp.